MISSING BODIES

Brian Marriner is a prolific writer and one of Britain's leading true crime authors. He regularly contributes to crime magazines both in this country and in the US, including *True Detective*, *True Crime Monthly* and *Master Detective*. He has written several editions of *Murder Casebook*, has been a collaborator on many books, and has made appearances on both TV and radio. He is currently the author of five published works, including the novel *A Splinter of Ice*. An expert in criminology and forensic science with an encyclopaedic knowledge, his book *Forensic Clues to Murder* was described by Colin Wilson as 'the definitive text on forensic medicine, which is destined to become a modern classic.' Brian Marriner lives in Yorkshire.

By the same author

A Splinter of Ice
Forensic Clues to Murder
Cannibalism, The Last Taboo!
Crimes of the Heart

MISSING BODIES

Brian Marriner

arrow books

First published by Arrow Books 1994

1 3 5 7 9 10 8 6 4 2

Arrow Books Limited
Random House UK Ltd, 20 Vauxhall Bridge Road, London SW1V 2SA

Random House Australia (Pty) Limited
20 Alfred Street, Milsons Point, Sydney,
New South Wales 2061, Australia

Random House New Zealand Limited
18 Poland Road, Glenfield
Auckland 10, New Zealand

Random House South Africa (Pty) Limited
PO Box 337, Bergvlei, South Africa

Random House UK Limited Reg. No. 954009

A CIP catalogue record for this book
is available from the British Library

ISBN 0 09 930318 3

Printed and bound in Great Britain by
Cox & Wyman Ltd, Reading, Berkshire

CONTENTS

For Ruari, Gabriel and Colin – good friends in bad times.

INTRODUCTION

The immediate problem facing any murderer is the disposal of the body of his victim. The typical killer leaves the body where it falls, but a small core of cold and calculating killers plan to get away with their deed. They reason that if there is no body, then there is no proof of guilt. This is a fallacy which has sent many a murderer to the gallows.

John George Haigh, for example, disposed of his bodies in acid and told the detective who arrested him: 'Mrs Durand-Deacon no longer exists. She's disappeared completely and no trace of her can ever be found again . . . I've destroyed her with acid . . . How can you prove murder if there's no body?'

As it happened, it was quite easy. The victim's acrylic dentures were recovered from the sludge at the bottom of the vat of acid at Haigh's factory, along with her gallstones. Once on remand in prison, Haigh began regaling fellow prisoners with his theory that murder could not be proved without a body, explaining: 'Because there would be no *corpus delecti*.' From then on, they called him 'Old Corpus Delecti' with humorous contempt.

The real legal situation is that *corpus delecti* is a Latin phrase meaning – literally – 'the body of the crime'. It includes every aspect of an alleged crime: the circumstances, direct and indirect – or circumstantial – evidence, which alone can convict a person of murder without any corpse, providing that it is strong enough to convince a jury that murder has taken place and the accused person has committed the crime.

For example, if a man were seen by witnesses throwing his wife into a raging torrent, the body being swept away downriver and lost, that alone would be proof enough of murder.

The various methods used by killers to hide the body of their victim run the gamut from acid to arson, burning to burial. Most bury the body in a shallow grave; some sink it in deep water, weighted down. But bodies have a habit of surfacing . . . James Camb disposed of Gay Gibson's body at sea. Brian Donald Hume dropped the dismembered body of Stanley Setty into the sea from an aeroplane. Dennis Nilsen cut up some of his sixteen victims and flushed them down the toilet, others he burned on a garden bonfire.

The main reason for such elaborate disposal of the body is that in most cases the identification of the body leads straight back to the killer. For this reason, killers have gone to extraordinary lengths to hide the identity of the victim, even skinning and beheading them, as in the 1986 case of the torso found in Ashdown Forest, Sussex. The press dubbed it the 'Body with No Name' case. The head and hands were missing, and the body had been skinned like a rabbit. But good forensic work led to the identification of the victim as Latifa Lazaar, younger wife of Kassem Lachaal. On 24 March 1988 Lachaal was duly convicted of the murder at Lewes Crown Court and sentenced to life imprisonment.

There have been only six cases this century in England of a conviction for murder without a body. The first was the *Veronica* mutineers' murders in 1902. The second was a man named Davidson, convicted in 1934 of the murder of his baby son, although no body was ever found. His confession to disposing of the body by burning it on a fire at a refuse dump was accepted. Then there was James Camb. The fourth case was that of the Hosein brothers, convicted in 1970 of the kidnap and murder of Mrs Muriel McKay, wife of a newspaper executive. Her body was never found, and it is believed that the brothers fed it to pigs on the farm they owned. Then came the case of Iam Simms, charged with the murder of Helen McCourt in Merseyside. Helen's body was never found, but blood on Simms' clothing was subjected to the DNA genetic fingerprint test, and when compared with blood from Helen's parents, the conclusion was that the blood was 126,000 times more likely to come from an offspring of the parents than from a random member of the population. As a result of this DNA test 'by proxy', on 14 March 1989 Simms was sentenced to life imprisonment for murder. The latest and sixth 'no body' case took place in Huddersfield, when a Moslem couple vanished from their home, leaving it like the *Marie Celeste*, with all their belongings still there. On 17 December 1991 two brothers of the missing woman were convicted of both murders and jailed for life.

In addition to the English cases, we have the classic Irish case of the matricide Edward Ball (1936), and two cases in Wales – Michial Onufrejczyk, who killed his partner in 1953, and Martin Ryan, who murdered his wife in 1990. And there is the case of L. Ewing Scott, convicted in the United States in 1957 for the murder of his wife.

Obviously, in any murder trial without a body, the prosecution labours under a handicap. In the absence of a confession or physical evidence, the jury will want to know *why* the accused should have murdered the alleged victim. Under the law, there is no onus on the prosecution to prove motive in any criminal trial. This is simply because in many cases no motive is apparent, and we call them 'motiveless' murders, which is false. Every killer has his reasons, but in some cases those reasons are too weird to be capable of any logical explanation. The real motive could only be discovered by a psychiatrist – if then.

However, motive – along with method and opportunity – provides the classic clue with which a detective investigates any murder. 'Who gains?' remains a valuable question in detection. It was Fryn Tennyson Jesse, in her book *Murder and Its Motives* (1924), who gave us the definitive six categories of motive. They are: Elimination, Gain, Revenge, Jealousy, Lust and Conviction. They remain pretty comprehensive to this day.

Camb killed for the purpose of elimination, Ball from conviction – madness being a form of conviction that the victim must die – and Onufrejczyk from greed: he wanted his partner's share of their farm.

But what of Mark Chapman, who killed his idol, John Lennon? He killed to gain fame, and so his motive must have been a mixture of greed and jealousy. The problem of motive was seen in the trial of the Yorkshire Ripper, Peter Sutcliffe. Although Sutcliffe had confessed to the murders with which he stood charged, because the defence claimed insanity, the prosecution was obliged, in effect, to prove motive. The Attorney General posed the question to the jury, asking them to decide: 'Is he mad or is he bad?' They decided that Sutcliffe was bad, and he was duly convicted of murder.

Along with the facts, the prosecution has to adduce intent of some kind, even though it does not strictly have to prove motive. It certainly has to prove *guilty intent*. Every case of murder – indeed, any crime – is composed of two parts: *actus reus*, a Latin term meaning the physical act (of killing a person, in the case of murder), and *mens rea*, which means the intent, or literally: 'guilty mind'. In common law, the mere commission of an act does not of itself constitute guilt, unless the guilty intent is also present. The law does not prosecute a person for guilty intent alone, but only in such cases where the guilty intent has led to the commission of a crime. If the prosecution fails to prove intent, a murder charge may well be reduced to manslaughter – which surely would have been the correct verdict in the Camb case.

It is apparent that he did not go to Gay Gibson's cabin with murder in mind. He expected an easy seduction. But something went wrong in that cabin, which resulted in the girl being pushed out of the porthole, and the prosecution argued that *mens rea* – guilty intent – can be formed instantly. The girl resisted rape or sexual assault, and Camb strangled her as a result – or so the prosecution argued.

It does not seem to be a reasonable argument, based on the limited evidence in the case, and although the Crown may not have to prove motive, the ordinary reader will demand a reasonable explanation for a set of actions – and so will a jury. There have been many acquittals simply because the Crown could not show *why* the person in the dock should have committed murder.

In order to prove a murder without any body, the prosecution has to rely on indirect – or circumstantial – evidence. The very term baffles many a student of crime, but quite simply, circumstantial evidence means evidence derived from facts not in dispute. The classic example is that of Robinson Crusoe, when he saw the footprint in the sand. He had not seen any stranger, but he knew beyond doubt that he was no longer alone on the island. Or as Thoreau put it: 'Sometimes circumstantial evidence is very strong, as when one finds a trout in the milk.'

Although circumstantial evidence has gained a bad name in some quarters, it is vital in murder cases, for the obvious reason that most killers commit the act only when they are sure they are not observed and there are no witnesses to the deed.

Throughout the centuries judges have been at pains to explain to juries that circumstantial evidence can be more important and truthful than direct evidence. Direct evidence – such as an eyewitness – may be tainted;

mistaken identity is a classic cause of the miscarriage of justice. But as Lord Coleridge observed during one trial almost a century ago, (and this was a poisoning case, the most difficult crime to prove because it is carried out in secret):

'This class of evidence is a network of facts cast around an accused man, and such a net might be a mere gossamer thread, as light and insubstantial as the air itself. It might vanish at a touch or, although strong in parts, it might leave great gaps and rents through which the accused is entitled to pass in safety. Alternatively, it might be so close, so stringent, so coherent in its texture, that no effort on the part of the accused can break through.'

So although circumstantial evidence is derived from facts not in dispute, the interpretation of those facts may often be disputed. The evidence against the recent cases of people freed from long prison terms – the Guildford Four, Maguire Seven, Birmingham Six, and so on – was mainly circumstantial. Convictions relied solely upon disputed confessions. As a result, there is now pressure on the English legal establishment to adopt the Scottish system, whereby no person can be convicted solely on the basis of a confession. There must be some kind of corroboration.

However, direct evidence of the eyewitness kind was responsible for the wrongful convictions of Timothy Evans, who was hanged in 1950, and Oscar Slater, whose 1908 death sentence was commuted to life imprisonment. One class of evidence cannot be preferred against another, but as F. Tennyson Jesse argued, while they may be misinterpreted, 'circumstances themselves do not lie'.

Missing bodies are not as rare as might be thought, and there are possibly many more murderers who would be brought to trial if only the body of the victim could be found. Lacking a body, and with very little circumstantial evidence, the police are often powerless to act. Although unsolved murders constitute less than five per cent of the annual total in Britain, it should be remembered that given an annual murder rate of around five hundred, that five per cent can add up to twenty-five cases a year . . .

Thousands of people go missing in Britain every year. Most are people running away from failed marriages or failed lives; others are due to loss of memory or mental illness. The exact figure is not known, but the Salvation Army deals with six thousands cases of missing persons a year, and experts believe the total figure may be as high as sixty thousand.

Most – some eighty-five per cent – eventually reappear of their own accord, but fifteen per cent – or four thousand people – vanish forever. It is likely that a small proportion of these are victims of secret murder. The figures for unsolved murders are never published, but are substantial. Mamie Stuart is a prime example.

This thirty-six-year-old woman vanished from her Swansea home just before Christmas 1919. Nothing further was heard of her, despite strong police suspicion against her husband, George Shotton, who was arrested and questioned. His garden was dug over before he was released. It was forty-three years later that potholers found the remains of the missing woman in a fifty-foot shaft on the Gower coast. She had been cut into three pieces – the thigh-bones sawn in half – but an engagement ring on her finger provided proof of her identity. An inquest had to be held, and a retired postman came forward to say he had seen George Shotton struggling with a heavy sack all those years previously. An urgent police search went out for Shotton, who was located in a Bristol cemetery. He had died in 1958, having got away with the 'perfect murder'.

The most notorious missing person remains Lord Lucan, but sudden vanishings are nothing new. In the Victorian era there were two separate waves of vanishings in the same district of London. The first was in

November 1881, when Urban Napoleon Stanger, who owned a baker's shop, vanished. It was commonly believed that his wife and her lover had murdered him, baking his body into pies – as in the Sweeney Todd legend – thus disposing of the evidence. In April 1882 a second wave of vanishings began, resulting in the disappearance of five people from the same district of London within a year.

Today, as with the case of Issei Sagawa, who ate his girlfriend in Paris in 1981, or the more recent Jeffrey Dahmer case in Milwaukee, USA, cannibalism seems to have become the favoured method of making a person vanish – by eating them!

However, the central fact to bear in mind is that modern law makes the conviction for murder without a body possible only where the circumstantial evidence is so 'cogent and compelling as to make guilt morally certain'. High standards indeed . . .

1
LIVERPOOL'S *VERONICA* MUTINY TRIAL

For almost three hundred years there had been no conviction for murder in England without a body. Sir Matthew Hale, a leading legal expert of the seventeenth century, had written the definitive textbook to which judges and lawyers alike deferred when considering points of law, and in it he advised that there should never be a conviction for murder or manslaughter where no body had been found.

Hale quoted two cases which had persuaded him of this proposition. The first concerned an uncle bringing up his niece, his heir under the law, who was punishing her for misbehaviour. The girl was overheard pleading: 'Good uncle, do not kill me.' She then disappeared. The uncle was committed for trial under suspicion of murder and was ordered to produce the child at the next assizes. Unable to find her, the uncle brought another girl to the assizes, of the same age and wearing his niece's clothing. However, the deception was discovered and the uncle was found guilty of murder and hanged. But the girl reappeared when she came of age, to claim her inheritance. After being beaten by her uncle, she had run away from home and taken refuge with strangers . . .

Then there was the case of a man called John Miles, who was hanged for the murder of his friend William Ridley, with whom he had been drinking, and who had later disappeared. After the execution it was found that the 'deceased' Ridley had fallen, while drunk, into a deep privy and drowned. No one had thought of looking for him there.

Hale had tremendous influence over judges, his book becoming their bible. The rule of Hale was even used in the case of a mother and reputed father of a bastard child, who were seen to strip it and throw it into the dock at a seaport town. The body was never recovered, but the judge advised an acquittal on the grounds that 'the tide might have carried out the living infant'.

The effect of such a rule was to protect from prosecution any killer who had been clever enough to dispose entirely of his victim. This was bad law, but no judge likes to create a precedent. That Hale's rule had ended was seen in 1934 when a man called Davidson was convicted of the murder of his small son, having confessed to burning his body to ashes in a fire at a refuse dump. Cases like that of Davidson, and later Camb, came to be used as precedents, and convictions for murder without a body became more frequent as a result. But the case which created the precedent was that of the *Veronica* mutineers in 1902. Seven men were murdered and their bodies never recovered, yet guilt had to be proved to preserve the rule of law.

It was a plain case of piracy and murder. The very word 'piracy' is filled with romantic associations: flashing blades on the Spanish Main, the skull and crossbones. In fact, piracy does not necessarily involve capturing another ship and can be effected by violently seizing a ship from its lawful owners, as happened in this case.

Piracy was used in the charges against the defendants because it was the technical and legal term for what transpired, but to the man in the street it was a plain case of mutiny and murder. There was – and can be – no excuses for the *Veronica* mutineers. In its way it remains baffling, since never has such a revolting crime – the brutal murder of seven men – been committed with so little reason. In fact, no reason was advanced; it was a precursor of the modern 'motiveless' murder . . .

The 1,100-ton sailing ship *Veronica* was a British vessel from Liverpool which traded from South America, regularly calling at ports in the United States, Mexico, Argentina and Brazil. In late 1902 she sailed from Ship Island in the Gulf of Mexico, bound for Montevideo, with a cargo of timber. The trip was expected to take between sixty and seventy days, depending on winds, and enough provisions had been taken aboard for the crew of twelve.

Captain Alexander Shaw, an American, had signed on crew members as the vessel was being loaded. His first officer was Alex MacLeod, a tough disciplinarian who wouldn't hesitate to knock a man down if he didn't respond to an order quickly enough.

Captain Shaw had a somewhat dubious reputation himself, making a practice of recruiting seamen from the dregs of the waterfront. In the late 1880s he had been arrested in Boston for cruelty to his sailors, but was released on five-hundred-dollar bond. He fled from the court's jurisdiction.

For the October 1902 trip he had a very mixed crew. Willem Smith – real name Dirk Herlaar – was a Dutchman. Alec Bravo was a native of India, living in Scranton in the United States. There were three Germans: Harry Flohr, eighteen, Gustave Rau, twenty-eight, and eighteen-year-old Otto Monsson; and three Swedes: Gus Johansen, Julius Herrson, and Fred Abrahamson, the second mate, who had a very bad reputation as a brute. Pat (Paddy) Durran was the sole Irishman, and finally there was the ship's cook, thirty-year-old American Negro Moses Thomas. He was to become an important witness for the prosecution.

The ship sailed on 6 October; by 8 December a mutiny had resulted in seven members of the crew – including the captain – being killed and thrown overboard. The affair first came to light when the SS *Brunswick*, a

British tramp steamer, anchored off Cajueira Tutoia, a small island off the north coast of Brazil, to pick up a cargo of cotton. It was 28 December 1902, and the chief officer, William Watson, noticed a ship's lifeboat bearing the name *Veronica*.

There were five men abroad, all weak and exhausted. They were Smith, Rau, Monsson, Flohr and the cook, Moses Thomas. Humanitarianism is the rule of the sea, so Watson agreed to take them on board. Rau, the spokesman for the five, explained that they were the only survivors of a fire at sea when the *Veronica* had blazed out of control.

They had had to take to the lifeboat with just a barrel of water and a few biscuits. They had spent five days in the boat before reaching land on Christmas Day, and were starving and exhausted. Mr Watson wanted to know what had happened to the rest of the crew. Rau had rehearsed his story well and had drilled it into his companions. The trip was a catalogue of disaster, he said. On 25 October Gus Johansen died at sea. On 23 November another accidental death occurred when the first officer, MacLeod, fell from the main topsail-yard.

Finally, on 20 December, there was a fire. The captain gave the order to abandon ship, so Rau and his men took one boat, the captain and the rest of the crew another. The boats had become separated in the thick smoke and Rau did not know if the others had survived.

Mr Watson was not completely satisfied. He wanted to know if the *Veronica* had been burning badly when they left her. 'Yes,' Rau replied. 'She was in flames aft.' Then how had they managed to get the lifeboats from aft? And why take only eleven biscuits? Rau explained that they had seized whatever the cook had been carrying. Mr Watson informed his captain, George Brown, of the affair, and Captain Brown entered Rau's version of events in the ship's log.

Accommodation was prepared for the survivors, and the captain told them that he would hand them over to the consul at Lisbon for further assistance. He also had the *Veronica's* lifeboat hauled aboard, noting that it had been newly caulked.

On the trip to Lisbon Captain Brown suspected something odd about the party. The cook, Moses Thomas, was evidently afraid of the others, because he begged to be berthed separately. On 2 January 1903, the captain asked Rau how he had managed to navigate the lifeboat. Rau said he had no compass, so he steered by the stars. He pointed to the two visible in the sky – but, as the captain knew, they would have taken him east by north-east – *the wrong direction*.

The crew of the *Brunswick* were also keen to hear the survivors' story, and they too were quick to spot discrepancies. Smith, who confirmed that the fire had started in the captain's cabin, was carrying a suit of clothes – yet none of the men had had time to grab their seaman's caps. One of the men had stockings belonging to Captain Shaw. How had he managed to rescue them from a blazing cabin?

Monsson and Flohr offered no reply to these queries, and when a persistent seaman called Templeton asked how all three Germans had managed to get into the same boat, they said they had all been on the same watch. To further questions they offered no reply, simply walking off.

The *Brunswick's* bosun, Frederick Standere, was even more persistent. He questioned Rau closely about the efforts made to put out the fire, and asked how the captain and the port watch had managed to launch lifeboats when, according to Rau's account, the *Veronica* had been blazing from the stern to the mainmast. Rau said – rather lamely – that he supposed the port watch had run along to windward aft, an explanation Standere received with incredulity.

The disclosure of the mutiny and murders came on 12 January, when the cook, who had been heard howling in the night and groaning, asked to see the captain. He confessed the full affair to Captain Brown, who wrote a report in his log. The entry for 21 January read:

> Moses Thomas of the barque *Veronica* . . . one of the shipwrecked crew on board this vessel, did on the 12th day of January, 1903, make a statement to me privately that the other four men, led by Gustave Rau, did, before the barque was burnt, kill the captain and mate and also attempt to kill him . . .

In Lisbon, the British consul ordered that the five men be taken on to Liverpool and handed over to the police. He telegraphed all the information about the case to the Liverpool City Police.

The *Brunswick* docked at Liverpool on 29 January, and was boarded immediately by Detective Inspector Duckworth, Detective Sergeant Ford and Detective Constable Inglis. The prisoners were confronted with Thomas's accusations. Flohr at first followed the false story, but quickly broke and made a full confession. The other three men made statements accusing the cook of having led the mutiny. Rau, Monsson and Smith were taken to police headquarters and charged with the murder of Captain Shaw and six others on the high seas.

The three prisoners stood trial on 12 May at the Liverpool Spring Assizes before Mr Justice Lawrance. The prosecution was led by Mr Tobin, KC, supported by F. E. Smith – later Lord Birkenhead. Mr Maxwell represented Rau; Mr Cuthbert Smith and Mr Russell appeared for Monsson, and Mr Aggs for Smith. The ten charges in the indictment included murder, conspiracy, arson, piracy and theft.

The clerk of the court read out ten charges; the last one was:

> On the eighth day of December, 1902, and on other days thereafter, on board the British ship *Veronica* on the high seas, [they – Rau, Monsson and Smith] feloniously did

commit theft at the time of committing the crime of piracy in respect of the ship: to whit, violently taking the said ship from the possession and control and against the will of Alexander Shaw, master of the said ship.

The prosecution proceeded with the case of the murder of Captain Shaw alone, but brought in evidence relating to the other charges to establish proof of guilt. Mr Tobin, in his opening speech, set out the facts of the case, saying that the mixed nationality of the crew was an important element. He said that the fact that all the defendants were Germans was also 'significant'.

Mr Tobin said the motive for the crime lay in the belief of the prisoners that their officers had been harsh towards them. 'I must say at once, so far as the evidence in this case goes, there appears to have been no solid foundation for this feeling. They brooded over these not very substantial grievances and worked themselves up to such a pitch that they determined to get rid of their officers.' He added that as the rest of the crew had been witnesses to the murders, they had to be killed too.

Rau threatened Flohr that if he didn't join in the mutiny he would go over the side. Rau, the ringleader, first hit Paddy over the head with a belaying pin, knocking him senseless and shutting him into a locker. When the first officer, MacLeod, came looking for Paddy, he too was knocked senseless and was immediately thrown overboard.

Rau and Smith had gone to deal with the occupants of the aft cabin, leaving Flohr to guard Paddy. A couple of seconds later, Flohr heard two shots and saw Rau and Monsson carrying revolvers. Then Abrahamson staggered in the direction of the captain's cabin, crying out that he had been shot.

The man at the wheel, Johansen, was struck down by Flohr on Rau's orders, but he got to his feet and ran away. He ran into Rau's revolver and begged Rau not to kill him. Rau threw him overboard, telling Flohr to take the wheel. In the midst of this mayhem, the captain appeared on the scene, calmly studying the compass, not having noticed a new man at the wheel.

He truly must have been deaf. Rau threw a belaying pin at him, causing him to stagger, and then shot him twice. The captain managed to drag himself away, falling down the steps to the navigation cabin, where he locked himself in. When he attempted to reason with Rau, he was shot at again. The captain and second mate, Abrahamson, both wounded, were thus imprisoned in the aft cabin.

Flohr left the wheel to go and see what Rau was doing. Up on deck he saw Monsson standing next to a window, beneath which lay a very large pool of blood. Monsson explained that Julius Herrson had tried to escape via the window, and he had hit him with a belaying pin and thrown him overboard.

Now came a moment of farce amid the carnage. Paddy recovered consciousness and came staggering out of the locker where he had been thrown. He went up to Rau, his face covered with blood, and begged for a drink of water. Rau said: 'All right. I'll give you a good drink.' He struck Paddy again over the head and had him thrown overboard. There were now three men overboard: MacLeod, Herrson and Paddy Durran.

The Negro cook, Moses Thomas, had locked himself in his cabin and refused to come out.

'Come out, you son of a bitch,' Rau shouted at him. 'There's nothing left but you!' All night Rau raged outside his cabin. Early next morning, Rau ordered him to come out or be killed. Thomas came out and Rau levelled his revolver at him, but Smith intervened, saying: 'Don't kill him. He's done nothing to you.' Rau decided to spare the cook, ordering him to make breakfast.

After breakfast, the mutineers barricaded the wounded captain and second mate in their cabins by locking their doors and nailing boards over the skylights and other exits. The intention was to starve them out, and they stayed there for the next few days, injured and without food and water. The cook took his turn both at the wheel and in pumping ship.

There was some confusion over how long the captain and second mate were actually imprisoned, one witness saying three days, another a week. But on the third day Rau took the cover off the skylight and looked down at the captain who, in agony, wounded in the neck and stomach, begged Rau to give him water.

'I'll give you my gold watch. Please save my life. I have got a wife and children and I should like to see them again.' Rau struck a bargain with him: he was given water in exchange for maps and a sextant.

The second mate, Abrahamson, was lured out of his cabin into an ambush. He was struck on the head by Flohr and shot in the shoulder by Smith. He jumped overboard, and while he was swimming, Rau ordered the ship turned about. Then Rau, Smith, and Monsson all took shots at Abrahamson, who disappeared under the waves. Bravo, the Indian, was sent to drive out the captain with an axe – into the arms of his killers.

When Captain Shaw came stumbling out, Rau shot him through the temple and tossed him overboard. Rau, Smith, Monsson and Flohr now ransacked the captain's cabin, taking money, clothing and other items. Rau took the gold watch.

Now Rau decided it was time for Johansen and Bravo to go. Smith shot Johansen; Flohr fired three times at Bravo, who leapt over the side and was drowned. The five remaining men could not sail the ship alone, so the cook was set to caulking the lifeboat. When ready, it was loaded with provisions and the men boarded it and set sail, first setting fire to the *Veronica*. When they sighted land they dumped the provisions and navigation instruments, acting the part of distressed sailors.

Following their arrest in Liverpool, the three prisoners made statements blaming the cook for the mutiny. They knew he had talked to the captain of the *Brunswick* and incriminated them, but, as the prosecution pointed out, had they kept silent, there would have only been Moses Thomas's word for the murders.

In making statements, they corroborated the cook's claim that seven men had been murdered and the ship deliberately fired to conceal the fact. If Moses Thomas had been the ringleader, then why would he tell the captain of the *Brunswick* the truth at the very first opportunity?

Flohr had originally been arrested and charged too, but after a few hours in a cell he made a second statement, backing up the cook's story, although he had had no opportunity to discover what the cook had said. The prosecutor said that he would not ask the jury to convict on the word of the negro alone, and it was for this reason that Flohr had been granted immunity to turn king's evidence, even though by his own admission he had taken part in some of the killings.

It appeared that the word of a crooked white man was preferable to that of an honest black one.

Ludwig Christian Heinrich Flohr testified on the first day of the trial. He said he had sailed previously on the *Veronica* under Captain Shaw without complaints. Rau and Monsson joined the ship two weeks after he had signed on, and both brought revolvers aboard. Rau immediately began talking of taking the ship over – before they had even sailed from Ship Island.

Once at sea, after some seven or eight weeks of sailing, Flohr was approached to join in the mutiny. He was on look-out when Monsson came to talk to him. Then Rau appeared on the scene.

'What did he say?' asked the prosecutor.

'He said: "I heard the chief mate and second mate telling how they were going to throw the two of you overboard." '

'Is that what Rau said?'

'Yes. Rau said that.'

'Did he say who the two were?'

'Monsson and me.'

'What else did Rau say after that?'

'He said we were to kill them and throw them overboard before they killed us. He said that he, Smith and Monsson were agreed to it already, and they wanted me to help them too. It was Rau who said that to me. I replied: "No, I cannot." Rau said to me: "Will you help us, yes or no?" I said "No. I can hardly see a pig killed, so how could I kill a man?" They replied that if I did not help them, I should go the same way as the others. I agreed, at last, through fear.'

'How many days was it altogether that the captain and the second mate were imprisoned in the cabin before they were killed?'

'About a week.' Flohr related the dreadful death of Captain Shaw, and how Rau rehearsed them all in the story of a fire at sea. At Lisbon, Rau got rid of the captain's gold watch and money by throwing them over the side of the *Brunswick*.

Cross-examined by Mr Maxwell, Flohr was asked: 'Is it your suggestion that Rau wanted to get rid of the officers?'

'Yes.'

'And this was three days before anything happened on that ship?'

'Yes.'

'Why did you not go to tell the captain?'

'I had no chance.'

'You were on board for three days after this?'

'Yes.'

'You had no chance of speaking to the captain, the first officer or the second officer?'

'No.'

'And you wish the jury to believe that?'

'Yes.' Denying that he had been rehearsed in his story by the cook, Flohr was cross-examined by counsel for all three defendants. When Mr Cuthbert Smith, for

Monsson, asked him how he came to get the new clothes he was wearing, he admitted that the police had supplied them. Mr Smith commented acidly: 'That is how you come to be better dressed than the men in the dock. You turn king's evidence and get better dressed?'

Moses Thomas testified on the second day, saying he was a native of Virginia and had been going to sea for ten years. His wage on board the *Veronica* had been forty dollars a month. He told of how, on the night the mutiny began, he heard shots followed by a man shouting: 'Oh Lord, captain! I am shot!'

He locked the door of his cabin and then heard Rau shout: 'I have killed the captain, the chief officer and the second officer, nobody left but the cook. Come out, you black son of a bitch, come out.'

He was forced to make coffee for the mutineers, but Rau made him drink it first in case he had poisoned it. Then came the fictitious story of the fire, invented by Rau.

'Who taught that story to the crew?' asked the prosecutor.

'Rau.'

'Did Rau say anything to you while you were learning it?'

'He used to hold a revolver to your head and say he would shoot you if you missed a word.'

Thomas said that Johansen and Bravo had been killed simply because they couldn't learn their lines. Flohr shot Bravo, who fell overboard.

'What happened to you?'

'Flohr said "Damn it!" and snapped his revolver at me twice and I ran under the fo'c'sle head. I came out and begged them not to kill me and they made me go down on my knees and take an oath. They said if I said anything against them there would be four against me, and they would be believed because they were white and I was black.'

Under cross-examination, Thomas denied that the crew never had enough to eat on the *Veronica*. He said

Flohr had definitely aimed a revolver at him and tried to fire, but the weapon had snapped twice as if faulty. He had not spoken to Flohr since. Rau was the last man to leave the *Veronica*, and the first to board the *Brunswick*. He agreed that he could speak and write English well, but denied that because of his command of English he had coached the others in the false story about the fire.

George Templeton, seaman on the *Brunswick*, testified that he had talked to the survivors of the *Veronica* and their story was that they had to leave their ship in such a hurry that they left their caps behind. Templeton then pointed to Smith, who had been carrying a suit of clothes, and said he thought it strange that he had had time to find a suit, but could not find his cap.

Detective Inspector Robert Duckworth testified about arresting Flohr, Rau, Smith and Monsson, having confronted them with Thomas's evidence. Rau's statement in reaction was read out in court:

> After a couple of days at sea the chief mate hit Smith. Not very long after that he hit at Harry Flohr. The second mate wanted to use Monsson and Flohr like a woman. I seen the second mate in the lazaret with Monsson with his head in a sail and he wanted to bugger him. I said to him: 'You mustn't do that, boatswain, it isn't good. I will report you if you do it again.'

Rau claimed that Thomas had started the mutiny by firing at the captain and second mate, who shot back. 'The steward shoots with his revolver . . . we was frightened for our life.'

After taking over the ship, the cook appointed Rau as captain, but when Rau wanted to spare the captain and second mate, Thomas callously shot them and ordered the rest of the crew to set fire to the ship. Flohr's original statement, the one he had retracted, read exactly the same.

Otto Monsson's statement was read out by the clerk

of the court. It was substantially the same account. He claimed that the second mate had been violent towards him and blamed the cook for the mutiny, claiming that Thomas had said of the captain and second mate, barricaded in their cabin: 'Let them die from hunger.' He ended by declaring:

> Gentlemen, we have not done anything wrong, for we fought for our lives. If the gentlemen who go to far distant lands, where one lives his life every day in constant insecurity and who may read this story, they will be able to say if it is right or wrong. I am eighteen and a half years old. I accept whatever punishment is allotted to me.

Willem Smith's statement was read out next. He related how he had signed on the *Veronica* in Biloxi, Mississippi. He said that when the first mate hit him, the cook said: 'Kill the bastard.' 'To which I said that I was not going to get in prison for the first mate.'

He too alleged that the second mate had wanted to use Flohr and Monsson as women. 'I frequently noticed that Paddy wanted to commit immoral assaults on Flohr. The second mate was tarred with the same brush as Paddy, and he frequently threatened to commit immoral acts with Flohr and Monsson. He even threatened to tie their hands and to wrap their heads in canvas, and with other acts of force get the better of his victims, who sometimes stood defenceless before this big and strong monster.'

Smith complained that the food had been 'vile' on board ship, and that Captain Shaw had once thrown his meal overboard, declaring: 'This is no food for a dog, much less for a human being.'

Smith also said that he had been knocked unconscious by the first mate and knew nothing of any murders until he regained his sense and asked Rau, Monsson and Flohr where the rest of the crew were. 'Rau told me that the first mate had jumped over the side and they told me the captain had fired a revolver which wounded Johansen, who also jumped overboard. They lauded the actions of the cook and his brave conduct.'

He claimed the cook had been in control at all times, issuing orders and telling the captain and second mate what their fate was likely to be. His statement went on: 'Afterwards it was arranged that the cook should act as captain; he appointed Rau mate, and we had to do as we were ordered.' It was the cook, too, who had ordered the *Veronica* to be set on fire, despite Rau's objections.

Smith really had been suffering from a head wound when he was picked up by the *Brunswick*. Now the medical officer of Walton Prison, Dr Price, testified about his examination of Smith's head wound, which had scarred over. Smith told him he had got the wound when Rau accidentally hit him with a belaying pin. Rau had intended to hit the first mate.

Rau went into the witness box on the third day, saying it was the cook who had warned the crew that the officers planned to kill them. (This was a fantastic story, since if the officers had indeed killed the crew, they would have been unable to sail the ship.) He related how the mutiny had started; he, Monsson, Willem Smith and Alec Bravo had been in the fo'c'sle when Julius Herrson went out to make water. They heard him fall and rushed out.

'I saw the chief mate. He had in one hand a belaying pin, and in the other hand a knife. I found a chain hook on the deck and threw it at the chief mate. The chief mate went over the side, and I heard the steward shouting.'

'You mean the cook?' asked his defence counsel.

'Yes sir. He says: "Fellows, here I am." The cook shot at them.'

Rau said the crew drove the officers aft with belaying pins, then secured them in their cabins by fastening rope around the doors. He was asked: 'Did you take a revolver on board with you?'

'No sir.'

'Who had a revolver on board?'

'I saw one on the cook.'

'How long were the captain and second officer in their cabin?'

'One and a half days, sir.'

Then Rau slipped up in his testimony. He said: 'I know a bit about navigation.' The judge was very interested in this statement and had him repeat it. It implied that only Rau could have navigated the lifeboat and thus the cook could not have planned to fire the ship and take to the boat.

Rau insisted that the 'nigger' had made up the fictitious story they had to learn – 'because he talked good English and I did not talk it so good.'

'Is it true that Alec Bravo was killed because he could not remember the story?' he was asked.

'Not exactly. There was more reason after that.'

Cross-examined by the prosecution, Rau was asked why he hadn't told the truth about the affair as soon as possible. He said he had been waiting until he got to Liverpool to do that.

Mr Tobin asked him: 'You got on board the *Brunswick* and there were white people there. Why did you not give the cook up to the captain of the *Brunswick?*

'Well, that was a tale made up by the cook. It was intended that we should have no trouble at all, and so everybody trusted him.' He admitted having hitherto lied to the captain of the *Brunswick* and to the police, and was asked by an incredulous prosecutor: 'Did the cook really give all the orders on the *Veronica?*'

'Yes, he played captain. The nigger put the captain's clothes on.'

'You obeyed the cook?'

'Yes sir.'

'Were you quite friendly with the cook in the lifeboat?'

'Yes.'

'Friendly with the man you thought was a murderer?'

'He saved our lives.'

Willem Smith then took the stand. Under cross-examination he was asked: 'Did you obey the cook's orders, too?'

'I had to do it, sir,' he told the court.

'Did you mean to give the cook up when you landed because he was a murderer?'

'Yes, certainly,' he replied, so was asked:

'Why did you not give the cook up to the captain of the *Brunswick*?'

'It was time enough when I came to Liverpool,' he replied firmly.

Mr Tobin made the closing speech for the prosecution, a reasoned and logical examination of the evidence heard. 'There are some central facts in this case which the defence have not been able to attempt to displace. They have been unable to challenge the allegations from the Crown that seven deaths by violence occurred on board that ship – seven deaths out of twelve men on a small ship 186 feet long. How did these men come to die? The answer must be that they died at the hands of the survivors – either one, or more, or all.

'It is suggested that after the death of Paddy their blood was up, and their lust for blood overwhelmed their reason entirely.'

He disposed of the defence suggestion that the survivors fought back against officers determined to kill them, by saying: 'It is significant to remember that, with the exception of the prisoner Smith, not one of these four men, the three prisoners and Flohr, received a single crack or wound, and by Smith's own admission his wound was caused by a mistake by his fellow prisoner, Rau.

'Gentlemen, there is one other matter that may trouble your minds, and that is why the life of the cook was saved at all. I dare say he was a useful man to have on board the ship, just one of those mistakes that sometimes criminals do make, a mistake which has led to the detection of these murders.

'It is represented by the prisoners, and this is the defence, that the black cook is the guilty murderer. You have seen him. If the cook murdered any of these seven men, why did he open his mouth to the captain of the *Brunswick?* There is another most important thing that goes to show that the cook had no connection with these crimes, and that is that Flohr said it.

'Flohr, a self-confessed conspirator, says the cook is innocent; Flohr, who has every reason to have hostile feelings towards him because he caused his arrest for murder on arrival at Liverpool. What there is of good still left in Flohr compelled him to say that the black cook had no lot or part in any of these crimes.

'There is one great contradiction between the black cook and Flohr. The cook says he was locked up for three days, but Flohr says he cooked the meals regularly every day. There is another discrepancy which I want to deal with, and that is the cook says he was locked up for three days and during that time the captain and second mate disappeared.

'According to Flohr they were locked up for six days, and according to the prisoners they were locked up for a day and a half. When people are living in the midst of a tragedy like that one can hardly wonder that they lose count of days . . .'

Mr Maxwell, for Rau, made the most aggressive defence speech. He urged the jury 'not to convict on the word of that despicable creature, Flohr, a self-confessed liar, or the evidence of the cook, a murderer also. Mr Tobin told you this, his words are these: "It was not right that the jury should be asked to decide the case upon the evidence of one man, a coloured man, alone."

'Gentlemen, you *are* being asked to decide this case upon the evidence of a coloured man alone. Mr Tobin told you that the charge arose out of a conspiracy by these three men in the dock to murder the officers of this ship, the *Veronica*. What evidence is there of conspiracy? You have only got Flohr's evidence. The cook says he knew nothing of any conspiracy, and Rau says: "I never murdered the captain. I was no party to the captain's death."

'That is the question you are trying today. The second officer and the captain came forwards. A shot was fired. I suggest to you that the man who fired the shot was the cook. Who would be the most likely man abroad that ship to have a revolver? It is common knowledge that countrymen of the same race as Moses Thomas think nothing of carrying revolvers and they think nothing of using them.'

It was a defence of crude racial discrimination, ruthlessly and powerfully argued.

'Then what was the end of poor Paddy? Paddy asked for a drink of water. Do you believe that this man Rau said: "I will give you a drink of water" and gave him the final touch to the head? It is too ridiculous, too improbable that such an awful occurrence should have taken place.'

Maxwell argued that Flohr had been presented as a Crown witness because it would be wrong to rely on the word of one coloured man. Yet Flohr had called Thomas a liar, saying he had not been locked up for three days but had cooked the meals. Then he turned his attack on Flohr.

'You saw Flohr in the witness box. Flohr has been paid for three months twenty-five shillings a week by the Board of Trade. He is able to come before you in decent clothes, shaved; to look at him you would never think he is a sailor at all. Flohr comes before you and says: "I never fired at Alec Bravo." He says it was Rau who killed Bravo. What does the other witness for the prosecution, Thomas the cook, say? He says Flohr fired one shot at the coolie and it killed him. He then turns round and snaps his revolver at the cook. Now, gentlemen, are you on evidence of that sort going to send one of these men to the gallows?

'What took place exactly on that ship and how some of these men met their deaths, I do not think anybody could tell you accurately. If you notice, according to Flohr's story, he was the only man aboard that ship on his own showing who knew about the death of every single one of these men except one. You know, he was a most remarkable man. He was present at the death, according to his own account, of everyone but Julius Herrson. He was here, there and everywhere during this night.'

Then Maxwell switched his attack back to the cook. 'You know the cook and you have seen him in the witness box. Does he bear out Rau's story, and that of the other prisoners, that he was the one who invented the tale? Why, gentlemen, he is the only witness we have had in the witness box who can speak English fluently.'

Then, Mr Maxwell alleged, Thomas realized that his fabrication was not good enough to fool the crew of the *Brunswick*, who were asking awkward questions. 'So he says: "I will be the first man; I will be the first man to tell the truth; I will save my neck." '

Mr Maxwell looked sternly at the jurymen and said: 'I do ask you, before finding Rau guilty, that you will well consider whether it would be as safe to convict a dog, far less a man, on such evidence.'

Mr Cuthbert Smith, for Monsson, said: 'So far as the prosecution in this case have attempted to make out that charge against Monsson, their failure has been hopeless. It is because I consider that they so failed that I advised Monsson not to go into the witness box, to enable the prosecution, by means of skilful cross-examination to attempt – to *attempt*, I say, gentlemen – to bolster up a charge founded on the frivolous grounds of the ingenuity of Flohr, the informer . . . double liar he confesses himself to be; murderer he has been proved on the evidence of the poor black cook . . .

'Thomas says: "I never saw any sign of a conspiracy." And, moreover, Thomas says: "Never throughout the whole time I saw Monsson had he a belaying pin, revolver or other weapon in his possession. Never did I see him guilty of any act of violence." I say the whole case of conspiracy in this case against Monsson rests entirely upon the evidence of Flohr. Monsson served on the *Veronica* on her last voyage. Monsson had served in that ship for seven months, on splendid terms with the officers, the same officers, mind you, that Flohr alleges he conspired to kill. He was discharged from that ship on September first and, my Lord, has the discharge paper before him. It is signed "very good". It is signed by the dead man, Alexander Shaw, for whose murder he is being tried. It seems almost that the dead man yet speaketh.'

Mr Smith said the motive was probably that spoken of by Rau, witnessed by others, when he remarked: 'All rich people, all people of the position who live aft in the cabin, ought to be destroyed. We want a revolution in Germany.' Mr Smith commented: 'It was the dream of some anarchist, perhaps.'

Mr Smith urged the jury to believe the cook, who had said there had never been a conspiracy, rather than Flohr, who was 'an informer and participant in everything that took place on the *Veronica*'.

'I do not appeal to you for mercy in his case at all. I appeal to you for justice. I confidently ask you for his acquittal.'

Mr Aggs argued on behalf of Willem Smith that his client had been unconscious when the murders were carried out and he could not have taken part in the massacre. He went on to point the finger at Moses Thomas, saying: 'Has it ever occurred to you to ask why the cook has been preserved? Gentlemen, I say this is the reason. The cook was the man of power. The cook was the man who had the third revolver. (The other two being owned by the captain and first mate.) The cook, the Negro, the American citizen in receipt of wages to the extent of forty dollars a month – he is the man who would, in every probability, and who I say in fact had the third revolver upon that boat.' He too then asked for an acquittal for lack of evidence.

In his summing-up to the jury, Mr Justice Lawrance told them that it was not necessary for the prosecution to prove that each of the three men did some violent act towards Captain Shaw. All that had to be established was whether all three men had acted in concert with a common purpose. If they had, then it did not matter whose hand had killed the captain: each would be responsible.

He said that the defence suggestion that the officers were going to throw nine members of the crew overboard was ridiculous. 'Nor has it been disclosed by the defence as to what the officers were going to do after these men had been thrown overboard in regard to the sailing of the ship.'

The jury would have to decide whether the crew had acted in self-defence – the judge referred to the men standing round the cabin with belaying pins in their hands, while the captain and second mate came out like rats in a cage.

The jury retired at 8.45 p.m., returning at 9 p.m. with verdicts of guilty of murder against all three prisoners, but with a recommendation of mercy on behalf of Monsson on account of his youth and previous good character.

The judge said he agreed with the recommendation and would forward it to the proper quarter. He then sentenced all three of them, Rau, Smith and Monsson, to death. By tradition, for the act of piracy the mutineers should have been hanged at Execution Dock at Wapping 'until three tides passed over them', but in this case Rau and Smith were hanged at Walton Prison. Monsson was reprieved.

There can be no doubt that Flohr was lucky not to find himself in the dock with the others, since he had been equally culpable, and the practice of allowing one criminal to turn king's evidence in order to convict others is always a detestable bargain.

The *Veronica* case remains the most pointless and horrific mutiny of modern times.

2
THE SHARK ARM CASE

The Shark Arm case remains the strangest mystery in the annals of Australian homicide, and it began with a simple fishing trip by two brothers off Sydney's Coogee beach.

Bert and Ron Hobson owned and operated an aquarium in Coogee, which attracted a fair number of paying tourists. Consequently they were always on the look-out for new specimens to add to their collection, particularly sharks. It was on the morning of 18 April 1935 that they hooked a seven-foot shark, hauling it in on a stout line. To their astonishment and delight, the thrashing of the small shark attracted a much larger tiger shark, which promptly swallowed it in cannibalistic fashion. They had lost a seven-foot shark, inadvertently using it as bait, but they had captured a magnificent fourteen-foot tiger shark, which was destined to become the star exhibit in their show.

It was placed on view to the public in a suitably large tank, but from the start it appeared to be very sluggish, hardly moving. The brothers put this down to the trauma of being caught, and expected the shark to recover in due course. But it did not. Despite having oxygen pumped into its tank, it remained dull and apathetic, as if it had eaten something which disagreed with it.

On Anzac Day – 25 April – only a small crowd had been attracted to the seaside resort, and fewer still actually paid to go and view the acquarium's latest acquisition, the fourteen-foot tiger shark. This was mainly due to the fact that Australia was in the grip of a depression. Those spectators who visited the acquarium did so because it was a cheap distraction for their children.

The new shark proved to be something of a disappointment. It now seemed restless, endlessly and slowly circling its tank like a huge and sinister torpedo. Then, at about five o'clock, it appeared to go berserk, flailing the water with its tail and shuddering into a mad frenzy, hurling itself about the tank.

To the horror of the watching public, it suddenly vomited, disgorging something into the water which turned it into a hideous dark froth. The shark swam away, apparently much relieved. When the dark staining cleared, the viewers were revolted to see that the shark had vomited up a human arm, a rope trailing from its wrist. It was indisputably human, since a tattoo was clearly visible, and the fingers of the hand trailed in the water as if beseeching for help.

The police from Randwick police station were quickly sent for, and they had the shark removed while they searched the bottom of the tank for any more human remains. There was nothing to be found. The arm was removed to a mortuary for examination by Dr Coppleson, who was an authority on shark bites, having examined thousands of them in the course of his career. After studying the arm, he and the Government Medical Officer were quickly able to tell the police that no shark had bitten that arm off. It had been cleanly severed at the shoulder with a sharp instrument, which meant it was a case of foul play . . .

The unfortunate tiger shark was killed the following day, its stomach being cut open in the hope of finding more of the body from which the arm had come. There was nothing to be found. What the experts did discover was that it was the smaller shark which had swallowed the arm, not the larger shark which had swallowed both shark and arm.

The human arm had come from an unknown person, and had obviously been dumped in the sea, where it was seized upon for a meal by a hungry shark. That the shark was then swallowed by a larger shark, and that both, among the many thousands of sharks in the area, were caught, was a fantastic coincidence which proved a headache for the police. They had the task of identifying the person to whom that arm had once belonged.

The first and obvious question in any murder inquiry is: when did the victim die? Dr Coppleson was able to tell the police that the arm had been in the shark's stomach for about a week. Normally the powerful digestive system of a shark would dissolve anything within thirty-six hours; but in this case, since the shark had eaten nothing during its period of captivity, it was apparent that the normal digestive process had ceased from shock.

Identifying the owner of the arm proved relatively simple. The Criminal Investigation Branch preserved the tattoo from the arm – which depicted two boxers in fighting poses – and also managed to take the fingerprints of the unknown victim by carefully peeling minute pieces of skin from the fingertips and reassembling them in the laboratory, rather like a complicated jigsaw. It took a considerable time, but the prints were on file. They belonged to a petty criminal named James Smith, aged forty.

Smith had had various jobs throughout his career, including bookie, construction worker, billiards-marker and road labourer. Every time he was arrested he gave a different occupation. He had once been a promising lightweight boxer – hence his tattoo. He was already on the missing persons file, having been reported missing by his wife. She said her husband had left their Gladesville home to go fishing on 8 April – ten days before the capture of the shark – with someone whose name he had not mentioned. However, she did say that her husband was a close friend of a well-known criminal, Patrick Brady. And her husband had had some business dealings with a man called Reginald Holmes, who owed her husband fifty or sixty pounds. She formally recognized the tattoo as being her husband's, and the police enlisted the help of naval divers to try to find the rest of Smith's body. It was a hopeless task. Nothing was found, and all the police were left with was an arm. It was another remarkable coincidence that of all the parts of Smith's body, that particular arm with its distinctive tattoo had been found.

This gave the police pause for thought. Smith had been a burly man. He would not have been easily killed. His record indicated that he had lately been engaged in acting as a guard on a luxury motor launch named *Pathfinder*, owned by Reginald Holmes, which had been used for ferrying drugs from ships at sea to various isolated landing spots on the shore. Opium had been its main cargo, and the Harbour police had been trying to catch the launch in the act of illegal transactions for months. Then in April the launch had been mysteriously sunk – some said by a rival gang – leaving Smith without a job. An insurance claim had been made on the boat, then quickly cancelled before it could be processed. Obviously Holmes did not want anyone looking too closely into his business affairs.

The Criminal Investigation Branch now had to liaise with the Harbour Police and the Narcotics Division, since the murder had led them straight into the shady underworld of international drugs-smuggling. Sydney, lying midway between China and the West Coast of America, played a vital role in this trade. American Customs officers went through ships which came directly from China with a fine-tooth comb, while ships from Australia tended to have a relatively easy passage – hence the benefit of transferring opium from Chinese ships to Australian ones in the comparative safety of Sydney harbour.

The criminals involved in this business made hefty

profits all along the line; in Shanghai, Sydney, San Francisco and San Diego, all the various handlers took their cut. In fact, drugs were so profitable in a city like Sydney, with its hordes of unemployed people willing to do anything for a quick buck, that a small-scale war had broken out between rival smugglers. It looked very much as if Smith had fallen victim to these opium wars, in which boats were sunk and men maimed and even killed.

Reginald Holmes, the owner of the sunken launch *Pathfinder*, had been Smith's employer, and he, if anybody, would know about his likely fate. Some detectives were detailed to keep an eye on Holmes and find out all they could about his recent activities. Other detectives attempted to reconstruct Smith's last known movements. They quickly realized that Smith had lied to his wife: he had not gone out that April morning to go fishing, since witnesses were found who had seen him without any fishing tackle that day. He had obviously meant to meet someone on business which he wanted to keep to himself. Who was the mystery man he had seen – and who might have killed him?

Inquiries revealed that Patrick Brady had recently visited Holmes' house. The police were anxious to talk to Brady, but he had quickly moved out of his rented cottage at Cronulla, and had to be tracked down. Brady was known to the police as an expert forger of cheques, with a criminal record stretching back twenty years. Meanwhile, Holmes was questioned at his home at McMahon's Point, where he operated ostensibly as a boat-builder. He claimed that ever since the sinking of his motor launch, he and Smith had been blackmailed by another boat-operator by the name of Patrick Brady. Holmes never did say exactly what he and Smith were being blackmailed about, but he hinted that Brady had been responsible for sinking his launch, which meant he had been a rival in the same line of business. Holmes was certain that Smith had gone to see Brady on the day he vanished. Perhaps to sort things out face-to-face . . .

The Truth of 19 May reported:

> Operating along the theory that the body might have been carved up, and perhaps only the arm with the identifying tattoo had been consigned to the waves, the police dug up certain premises, dragged the bottom of the bay, searched the tide-washed rocks, scoured the sandhills, but all to no avail. The mystery was still as deep and as apparently insoluble as ever.

The Truth took great credit for having broken the story, writing in a later edition:

> Slowly the great case is developing, and soon another chapter will be written in a story which – first discovered by *Truth* – is now being featured on front pages of the newspapers of the whole world – the baffling case of the man with the tattooed arm.

Inquiries about Brady had led detectives to a barman at the Cecil pub who said he had last seen Brady drinking with a man answering Smith's description on the day Smith vanished. On the evening of 16 May, three weeks after that arm had been found, the police arrested Brady, who had been traced to a flat in Kirribilli, detaining him on a trumped-up holding charge so that while he was behind bars they could search his cottage at Cronulla at their leisure.

It wasn't so much what that search turned up as what it *didn't* turn up which was significant. Brady rented the cottage, Cored Joy, at Talloumbi Street, Cronulla, for thirty shillings a week, furnished. The landlord had a complete list of the contents. Missing was a large tin trunk and a mattress. An anchor had gone from the boat-shed, as had two heavy window sashweights. Missing from Brady's own boat were three mats and a long coil of rope. During questioning, the tough but quietly spoken Brady said he had last seen Smith with Holmes and another man at the Cronulla cottage on 9 April. Holmes emphatically denied knowing Brady, persisting in this denial even when brought face to face with Brady by the police. Yet he had previously told police that the same Brady had been blackmailing him . . .

Other witnesses had been traced. Taxi drivers reported having driven Brady to Reginald Holmes' house at McMahon's Point. The all-important links necessary in any murder inquiry were slowly being made.

By chance – another coincidence in this tale – Sir Sydney Smith, after Sir Bernard Spilsbury the most eminent pathologist in the world, happened to be in Australia attending a meeting of the British Medical Association in Melbourne. He made a holiday of it, travelling on to Sydney. Once the police were aware of his presence, they requested his assistance in what was proving to be a baffling case. Smith was to write about the case in his book *Mostly Murder* (1959).

Smith examined the arm and his report confirmed Coppleson's findings: 'I found that the limb had been severed at the shoulder joint by a clean-cut incision, and that after the head of the bone had been got out of its socket the rest of the soft tissues had been hacked away. In my opinion it was certain that it had been cut, and not bitten-off by a shark. The condition of the blood and tissues further suggested that the amputation had taken place some hours after death.'

Smith was asked by the police to make a tentative reconstruction of how the murder had taken place, or what the process of dismemberment had been. After study, he said that he believed that the body of Smith had been cut up on the mattress from Brady's cottage and the mats from his boat. The dismembered corpse was then stuffed into the tin trunk – but one arm would not fit in. The trunk was full. The killer then cut off the dangling arm and tied it to the trunk with rope, knotting one end tightly around the wrist. The entire package – blood-soaked mattress and mats, and the trunk – was then taken out to sea and dumped overboard in deep water. The trunk sank, but the arm worked free, to be snapped up by a shark, and eventually disgorged in the aquarium in Coogee. The hypothesis made sense, but it could not point to the killer.

Three days after Brady had been taken into custody, with his wife Grace bitterly complaining that he was innocent and was covering up for Reginald Holmes, the thirty-four-year-old Holmes stepped back into the picture; this time his role was that of a would-be murder victim. The Water Police noticed a speedboat zigzagging across Sydney Bay at speed and gave chase. For four hours the police pursued the boat, which was being piloted by a man whose face was covered with blood. Eventually the police launch *Nemesis* managed to board the boat, only to discover Holmes leaning exhausted against the wheel, blood running from a bullet wound in his forehead. It was actually a deep groove in his skull, caused by a bullet which had just grazed him, but like all scalp wounds, it bled freely. Holmes smelled strongly of alcohol. He requested bandages. Asked to account for his odd appearance and behaviour, Holmes gasped out a fantastic story. He said that as he left his home that morning, he had been shot at and wounded by a mystery gunman. Fearing for his life, he jumped into his speedboat and took off. When the police launch chased him, he had assumed it was his attacker coming after him to finish him off. It was a hare-brained story – particularly since no less than six police launches had been involved in the chase.

The police were convinced that Holmes had tried to commit suicide but had missed, the bullet from his .32 pistol merely glancing off his skull, and had then invented his melodramatic story to cover up his botched attempt to take his own life. After questioning him in hospital, where he spent four days recovering under police guard, the police persuaded Holmes to tell them that Brady had confessed to murdering Smith and dumping his body – inside a trunk – off Port Hacking, and that he had threatened to kill Holmes if he 'dobbed'. Brady had said: 'If I'm not able to get you, one of me cobbers will.'

Incredibly, the police allowed Holmes to return to his home following his release from hospital, satisfied that they had now heard the truth of the matter. It was an odd decision; he was the chief witness in a murder case and an attempt had been made on his life. To release him seemed to be asking for another murder attempt. Perhaps the police thought they would learn more by letting him go and seeing what transpired.

The night before the inquest on James Smith, which had been set for 13 June, a police constable on patrol at Dawes Point noticed a Nash car parked underneath the driveway leading to the Harbour Bridge. Its front door was wide open and the headlights were blazing. It was one o'clock in the morning, and the constable expected to find the car abandoned as he shone his torch into its interior. Instead, he saw Reginald Holmes slumped dead over the wheel. At first he thought the driver was drunk, but when he shook him he discovered that the man had been shot through the chest and groin at almost point-blank range.

Holmes had died at around ten o'clock the previous evening. A revolver casing beside the car led detectives to conclude that he had been shot by someone sitting in the passenger seat.

Normally the area would have been swarming with people at ten in the evening, yet no witnesses could be found who had heard the shots. This led detectives to conclude that the killer had carefully made his shots coincide with the passing of a train over the bridge. It meant, of course, that the killer must have been well known to the victim, to persuade him to drive to that spot.

The murder of Holmes left the police in a pickle. He was to have been their chief witness against Brady at his murder trial, but now they had two murder cases and no witnesses. Even the result of the inquest on Smith spoiled the police chances of getting a conviction.

The inquest began on 13 June, but after twelve days the Supreme Court handed down a writ to the coroner, ordering him to halt the proceedings. Mr Justice Halse Rogers had concluded that an inquest could only be held if there was a body to inquire about, and that an arm was not enough. 'A limb does not constitute a body,' he ruled. In giving his judgement, the judge said he had based his ruling on the English statute: '*de officio coronatoris*' laid down in the year 1276, adding: 'A body has always been essential for the holding of an inquest.'

The ruling may have been legally correct, but it was not long before a new ruling was made, as in the case of James Camb, for example. Just as murder can be proved without a body, so can an inquest be held on that presumed murdered body. However, although the police could still proceed with the murder charge against Brady, without a coroner's verdict of 'murder by person or persons unknown', they would have to present some very substantial circumstantial evidence indeed – and they simply did not have it. They had allowed their star witness to be murdered . . .

The trial of Brady did take place, in September of the same year, but all the prosecution could do was to produce witnesses who had vague recollections of seeing Smith with Brady on the day he disappeared. Brady himself frankly admitted that Smith had indeed come to see him at his Cronulla cottage on that day, 8 April, but said he left that evening with yet another launch-owner named Albert Stannard. Without any reasonable proof of guilt, the jury duly acquitted Brady.

The police were furious, and remained determined to crack the case, which had attracted wide newspaper publicity – notably from *The Truth* – which made them look fools. Convinced that both Smith and Holmes had been murdered by the same man, the police now put on offer a reward of a thousand dollars for any information, with CIB Superintendent Prior leading a huge team of detectives in an effort to finally solve the case.

Three weeks after Brady had been acquitted, the inquest on Holmes was held and a verdict of murder was found by the jury. As a result, two men were arrested and charged with the murder of Holmes. One was Albert Stannard, the boat-owner named by Brady, and the other was a burly dock labourer named John Patrick Strong. At their trial in Sydney's Central Criminal Court in December, it became evident that the police could offer no better evidence against them than they had presented against Brady. Both men had alibis, and they were duly acquitted on 12 December 1935, leaving the police with egg on their face and the Shark Arm case unsolved.

In the wake of the case many rumours circulated in the underworld of Sydney, where 'dobbing' – or informing to the police – was considered an offence so heinous that only death was an adequate punishment, and even then, the death had to be a slow and painful one. One theory was that Brady had indeed been blackmailed – but not by Holmes, as he claimed, but by James Smith. The day after Smith's disappearance, several people saw Holmes drinking with Brady in an atmosphere of genuine cordiality.

But the police had lost their trump card in Holmes. Was he silenced because he had been an accomplice in the murder of Smith, or because he was a rival in the drugs racket, or simply to stop him testifying against Brady? We shall never know. We do know that the widow of the murdered Holmes, Inie, said in court that she had asked her husband who he thought had murdered Smith. He replied bluntly: 'Brady did it. He put the body in a trunk, took it out in his boat, and dumped it overboard.' However, the hearsay evidence of a murdered man was not accepted as evidence.

On 30 October 1952, the house in which Holmes' widow was living caught fire and burned to the ground, killing Mrs Holmes in the process. The cause of the fire was never discovered.

Patrick Brady, a former member of the AIF in World War I, died in Concord Repatriation Hospital on 11 August 1965. An expert forger who had served several prison terms, there was nothing in his background or character to suggest that he was capable of murder.

This case was incredible by any standards, proving, as William Congreve wrote, that 'murder will out'. No writer of fiction would have dared to string together such a strange chain of coincidences. For the murder of James Smith to have been discovered, his arm had to prove impossible to fit in the trunk, and had to be amputated, before being cast into the sea. Then a shark had to be caught. A shark which had eaten another shark which had eaten an arm, the only part of Smith which could identify him, and a shark from among thousands. Then the shark had to have indigestion, and vomit the arm up in the presence of dozens of witnesses.

But despite these coincidences, which seemed like the work of some supernatural agency determined to make the murder of Smith known to the world, neither his killer nor Holmes' was ever convicted. This remains a case where the bad guys won and justice was denied.

3
EDWARD BALL: MATRICIDE IN IRELAND

The first sign of anything amiss came with the sight of a car parked awkwardly. The village streets of Shankill had never been designed to accommodate such vehicles. James Rafferty was delivering newspapers that morning, Tuesday, 18 February 1936, and his curiosity impelled him to walk over and examine the vehicle, a two-door baby Austin. The time was 8.45 a.m.

The scene was Corbawn Lane in Shankill, a small village on the east coast of Ireland, ten miles from Dublin and two miles from the seaside resort of Bray. Corbawn Lane is a cul-de-sac leading to the sea, the end blocked off by a barrier of earth and stone, with a narrow path beside it for the pedestrian wanting to get to the beach. From the way the vehicle was wedged between the barrier and the path, it was apparent that its driver had attempted to get past the barrier and down to the shore, but had misjudged the gap and got stuck fast. The driver's door had been left open, as had the sun-roof.

What Rafferty found made him hasten to the local Garda barracks. The interior of the car was covered in blood, and a blood-soaked towel lay on the back seat. Rafferty was certain some dreadful accident had taken place. Police officers came out to examine the scene, and it took six of them to extricate the car from where it was wedged. Apart from the many splashes of blood inside the car, the officers noted some on a tyre and on the ground beneath. Documents found in the car indicated that it belonged to Mrs Lavinia – or "Vera" – Ball, aged fifty-five, wife of a well-known Dublin doctor. The police went to interview Mrs Ball at her home at 23 St Helen's Road, Booterstown. It was a small detached house with a garage attached, and was well-furnished for the time. Mrs Ball had private means as well as a part-time job.

At 12.30 p.m. the officers found only the maid, Lily Kelly, at home. She was busy laying the table, explaining that Mrs Ball was expecting dinner guests. She said that Mrs Ball had two sons, but had lived apart from her husband since 1927. However, the younger son, Edward, aged almost twenty, had come to live with his mother on 13 February, having left his Dublin flat because he could no longer afford the rent. He had no occupation, but had vague aspirations to a career on the stage. The maid was distressed to learn about the car accident, and revealed something that had been troubling her: the son's clothing was heavily soaked and muddied . . .

The police took the opportunity to examine the clothing, and asked the maid about the relations between mother and son. They didn't get on, she confided. The police could not at this stage have suspected that most rare of all forms of murder: matricide, but they did have sufficient grounds for suspicion to make them return.

The officers returned at 6.30 p.m. with Chief Superintendent Reynolds in charge of the party. The maid's gossip had been enough to arouse his interest. This time they found Edward Ball at home. A pleasant and intelligent young man, he showed no surprise that the police should be asking about his mother's movements, and said he had last seen her at 7.45 the previous evening. She had driven away in her car, saying she would probably stay the night with a woman friend, or her sister. He had opened the garage door for his mother, and had closed the front garden gate after her.

Edward Ball said his father had told him that his mother's car had been found damaged at Shankill, with bloodstains inside. On hearing that a blood-soaked towel was also in the car, Edward commented: 'I wonder whether there would be more blood on it than if a person had cut their hand or had an accident.' He displayed no alarm or concern about his mother's possible fate, and said he expected her home that evening for her dinner guests. He had not been invited to join them and had no idea where his mother might be.

Asked if he had had a row with his mother recently, he said he had accidentally broken a cup the previous evening and his mother had shouted at him, but the incident had soon been over. He was asked about his own background, and explained that he had been forced to give up his Dublin flat because he could not afford to pay the rent of £1 out of his total allowance of £2 10s weekly – £1 weekly from his mother, and £1 10s from his father. He had thus been forced to move in with his mother on 13 February.

How had his mother taken this? he was asked. She had taken him in grudgingly, complaining in the presence of the maid that unfortunately he was in her charge until he reached the age of twenty-one. Relations between mother and son were obviously not normal.

Asked to account for his movements the previous evening, he said he had been reading all the time, until he went to bed. He said his mother had gone out wearing a red dress, blue and white checked coat and brown shoes.

Reynolds left the room at this point, returning from the kitchen with a pair of men's shoes, sodden and covered in mud. He placed them in view of the young man, then went upstairs to Ball's bedroom, where he retrieved a newspaper parcel containing wet and bloodstained linen. He then went back downstairs and showed these to Ball, who could offer no explanation for them. When asked why his mother's room was locked, Ball said his mother always locked her room when she went out, taking the key with her. Ball then agreed to the police forcing open the door.

The room was in darkness, the curtains drawn. An electric fire was blazing away, in an obvious attempt to dry a large wet stain on the carpet. The maid was asked to look in the wardrobe. The clothing that Ball said his mother had been wearing was in there. Missing was a rug from the floor.

Ball was questioned again, especially about his relations with his mother. He said they 'only suffered one another', his mother being highly strung and suffering from fits of depression which made her irritable. But he insisted they were fond of each other, and dismissed any suggestion that his mother might have committed suicide. 'She's a great fighter, with all her troubles,' Ball said.

Edward Ball was questioned again the following day, this time by Superintendent Dunleavy. The police had been busy checking Ball's movements and now had the facts to challenge his story. Asked to account for his movements for the whole of the previous day, he said he had been in Dublin for a job interview, afterwards calling at the theatre where he sometimes had small parts. He had gone to his former flat to collect any letters, then lunched in a café, before 'knocking around town' the rest of the day. He had visited his father's house, then returned home.

He had been seen leaving the house on the Tuesday morning with a suitcase, but he denied it. On his hands were cuts and scratches, which he said he had got 'fooling about' with friends. A deep cut on his right thumb he explained was caused when he was cutting bread and the knife slipped. But he was right-handed . . .

Taken to his bedroom, he was asked to account for a vest, coat and trousers, all heavily bloodstained. He could offer no explanation, not even for the bottle of patent stain-remover found in his room. Also found was a note from his mother reading:

> I want you to understand that if you stay here tonight I am going to Mrs Allen. You did the usual dirty trick, coming in at 12 o'clock last night; it has upset me. I am three hours late for my work, but what can I expect?

The police had discovered the details of two further calls which Ball had made on the Tuesday and which he had neglected to mention. One was to a chemist to buy the stain-remover. Another was to a friend's flat to leave a suitcase, which when opened was found to contain woman's clothing, heavily bloodstained, and bed linen. The friend gave police a possible explanation for the strained relations between Ball and his mother. Ball had complained that his mother opened his letters – a thing he could not forgive in anybody.

Meanwhile, the house had been thoroughly searched, and blood was found in the bedroom, the landing and stairs, the kitchen, the outside path, and on the garage floor, making it difficult to establish precisely where Mrs Ball had been killed. More than nineteen items in Mrs Ball's bedroom were bloodstained, including the bed-head, mattress, dressing table, bedside lamp, hot-water bottle and hand basin. There was blood in Ball's room, on the landing and stair carpets, the wallpaper on the stairs, and even on the kitchen curtains downstairs.

By 21 February, Ball had confessed knowledge of his mother's death, showing police the blood-soaked pillow from her bed, which he had hidden in a linen basket in the attic. His story was that he had found his mother lying dead on her bed, having cut her own throat with a razor blade. He had tried to hide the deed to protect her reputation.

Ball had not at this point been arrested, although the police were in the house and keeping careful watch on him. When he went upstairs to the toilet, an officer followed him and stood outside the door. It was then that Ball attempted suicide, throwing himself from the second-storey window and injuring a vertebra in his neck. Two suicide notes were found in his pockets, both telling of his love for his mother. One read: '*The events of the last two days have been unbearable, and I claim the right to take my own life.*'

After being taken to hospital, Ball was arrested and charged with murder.

The trial began on 18 May 1936 before Mr Justice Hanna, KC. Ball pleaded not guilty, seeming almost cheerful in the dock. The prosecution presented its case. Servants told of bad relations between mother and son. The mother used to scream abuse at Edward – 'lashing him with her tongue', as one put it. Edward never answered back. Mrs Ball's secretary said her employer was 'highly strung', and her son's return home had upset her. She used to quarrel with the boy, but the secretary had never heard him threaten his mother or argue back. At most he had said: 'Ah, Mother! Do stop!' Evidence was heard that Mrs Ball had once had a nervous breakdown.

Dr Ball testified that he had noticed mental instability in his wife shortly after their marriage in 1902. She had abused him in front of patients, invented fictitious phone calls taking him out into the country to see non-existent patients, and met patients at the door and advised them to seek medical help elsewhere as he was useless as a doctor. This had caused him to leave her in 1927. Edward had been sent to an English boarding school to be educated, and his father had him in the holidays.

Dr Ball said that he feared his wife had suicidal tendencies, since two members of her family had died by their own hand, and she was known to be a kleptomaniac. She was also given to long periods of depression, speaking to no one for weeks on end. As for Edward, he had first tried to commit suicide when aged thirteen, and Dr Ball blamed his wife for their son's condition.

In January 1936 Edward, then living with a friend in Dublin, had confessed to having suicidal feelings. In November 1935 Mrs Ball had a nervous breakdown and went into hospital, returning home in the December. On 13 February the following year Edward had come to live with her. The following day – the fourteenth – she had left Edward a note complaining about his coming in late and telling him to find alternative accommodation.

The evidence of Edward's guilt of the crime of matricide was laid out before the jury. She had threatened to kick him out of her house within a day of his moving in. At 7.10 p.m. the evening of her death, the postman had called at the house and Edward had signed for a letter, appearing quite normal. At 1 a.m. a motorist had picked up Edward hitch-hiking from close to where the car was found. Edward had given his name as Winter from Tunbridge Wells.

Inside the dead woman's house, police had found blood on a flower-bed, on a hatchet in a shed, and in the rooms of the house – particularly the mother's bedroom. Since at least four pints of blood had been spilled on the carpet, the prosecution maintained that the murder had taken place there. They had no body – despite dragging the sea and using aircraft to look for a floating body – but they did have blood, vast amounts of it.

Two motorists gave evidence of having seen the baby Austin car at the barrier just before midnight with a couple in it, the man with his arm around a woman. It was Ball, supporting the lifeless corpse of his mother.

Ball had made a statement to the police, after handing over the missing key to his mother's bedroom, which had been hidden in his shoe. He said that his mother had complained that life was worthless and she wished she were dead, having failed in her marriage and everything else. She had asked him to promise to 'do all you can to prevent people thinking me a coward'. He had thought nothing of it – until he found his mother dead on her bed. He said he had 'worked like a machine' to conceal the suicide, carrying the body to the car and driving it to where it was found. He had then dragged the body down to the sea and cast it adrift, the tide carrying it away. He opened the sun-roof of the car to get rid of the smell of blood.

The Dublin harbourmaster was called to testify about the tides. He said that a body put to sea at Shankill would be carried clear of Dublin Bay and drift across to the Welsh coast. He told of experiments which had been carried out by the police, who had put seven oil-drums attached to crates into the water at that site. Three had been washed back to shore, one drifted twenty miles down the coast to Wicklow, and one had been recovered from Ramsay Island in Wales. The other two were never found.

The prosecution proved, through its pathologist, Dr John McGrath, that suicide had not been the cause of death. The hair of the victim had been hacked through with the hatchet. And had Mrs Ball cut her throat on the carpet, she would have lacked the strength to get back on the bed and leave blood there. A defence pathologist disputed this, saying it was possible that Mrs Ball had cut her own throat, not bothering to lift her hair out of the way.

The defence called two psychiatrists. One testified that Edward Ball was mentally abnormal, with a foolish and immature outlook. He seemed indifferent to his mother's death and unable to understand the seriousness of being charged with her murder. The other psychiatrist confirmed this, saying that Ball was suffering from dementia praecox – congenital adolescent insanity – and was weak-minded and morally deficient. Yet all who knew Ball spoke of his pleasant and polite manner, and his obvious intelligence. This was far from being the picture of insanity painted by the defence. A prosecution psychiatrist, while agreeing that Ball suffered from adolescent instability, said he saw no signs of insanity in Ball.

In a sense it was insanity itself which was on trial – or the legal perception of that condition. All too often in criminal trials, the medical experts state their diagnosis of insanity, which the lawyers cannot accept. There has always been this gulf between the legal and medical definitions of insanity, best exemplified in the trial of Christie, when the defence psychiatrist was publicly ridiculed for suggesting that Christie might be insane, having slaughtered six women over a period of years.

Most countries have a legal system which accepts that an insane person is not responsible for his or her actions. The present law on insanity in most English-speaking countries derives from the McNaghten Rules, which were brought into law following the case of a lunatic called Daniel McNaghten, who in 1843 shot and killed the private secretary to Sir Robert Peel, mistaking him for the Prime Minister. After the case, in which evidence of the state of McNaghten's mind was heard, the Law Lords brought in what were to become known as the McNaghten Rules, which state that at the time of committing an offence and in order to prove insanity, it must be shown that the accused was labouring under such a defect of reason from disease of the mind as not to know the nature and quality of his act, or if he did know it, that he did not know that what he was doing was wrong.

Although the McNaghten Rules are still in effect, under the Homicide Act of 1957 the defence of diminished responsibility was introduced, which reduces a charge of murder to one of manslaughter, providing the defence can establish that the accused was suffering from 'such an abnormality of mind' as to substantially impair his mental responsibility for his acts. This clause, like the McNaghten Rules, only applies to murder cases, and was brought in two years too late to save Ruth Ellis, the last woman to be hanged in Britain.

The judge displayed obvious sympathy toward Ball in his summing-up, and the jury, who came back to ask a question about the length of Mrs Ball's hair – it was elbow-length – took five hours to find Ball guilty but insane. *Even without the evidence of a body.* Ball looked dazed as he was sentenced to be detained in a secure mental hospital. What the jury did not know was that in November 1935, Ball had gone to the theatre with which he was associated to watch a dramatized version of Dostoevksy's novel *Crime and Punishment*, in which an old pawnbroker is murdered with an axe . . .

4

JAMES CAMB: THE PORTHOLE MURDER

James Camb cut a dashing figure in his white dress uniform as he stood on the deck of the luxury Union Castle liner *Durban Castle*. Aged thirty-one, thick-set and with a ruddy complexion, mischief sparkled in his dark eyes.

But he was no glamourous captain, or even the first mate. He was a lowly promenade deck steward whose duties were to cater for the whims of the passengers. He had a wife and young daughter back on dry land in Glasgow, but the sea was his occupation. He had served on merchant ships for fourteen years. And there was a dark side to James Camb: he made a practice of preying on lonely young female passengers, his attentions becoming sometimes so persistent that he had assaulted three young women on separate occasions; one had had to eject him from her cabin by force . . .

The *Durban Castle* was headed for Southampton, having left Cape Town on 10 October 1947. Now, a couple of days out from port, the ship glided through the waves at almost eighteen knots, the bow-wave parting elegantly before her. It was ninety miles to the nearest land, on the west coast of Africa, through tropical shark-infested waters.

The ship was almost empty, with only fifty-seven first-class passengers, but these were the days of austerity following the war, and most of the passengers were elderly expatriates returning to England. For them this was no pleasure cruise.

There was also a young actress, Gay Gibson, aged twenty-one. Born Eileen Isabella Ronnie Gibson in India on 16 June 1926, as a young child she was sent to England to be educated, her parents having to move about a good deal for her father's job. They had lived in Persia and India, among other countries.

Eileen – or 'Gay', as she preferred to be known – was still in England when war broke out and was called up for military service in 1943 at the age of seventeen. Posted to the Special Intelligence branch of the ATS and working at the War Office, Gay, who longed for a career in the theatre, got herself transferred to a touring revue company of service personnel, called 'Stars in Battledress', and toured the world with them, learning her craft.

She applied for a compassionate discharge in order to join her father in Durban, South Africa. This was granted, and on 12 March 1947 she arrived in South Africa together with her mother. However, she had to have a medical prior to discharge, in the course of which a chronic ear infection was noted, but she was graded AW1 – the highest medical fitness. The question of her fitness is important, since it was later to be claimed that poor health had led to her death.

Once in South Africa, Gay Gibson found herself in demand. She was young and pretty, a competent if not talented actress with professional poise. Her looks alone were sufficient to secure her employment. After some success in broadcasting and on the stage, Gay moved to Johannesburg, where work was more plentiful.

She toured with the Clifford Odets play *Golden Boy*, which also featured Eric Boon, former British boxing champion, in the cast. Although a success, the play was taken off after the theatre was condemned as a fire hazard. Gay had made friends among the cast – but three of them were subsequently to give evidence on behalf of the man charged with her murder . . .

Although the producer of the play had plans to take it to Pretoria, Gay announced her decision to quit and to return to England by the next ship. It was a fatal decision, a voyage to her death. But Gay had discovered that she was pregnant.

For Gay it was at first a long and dull sea voyage. She usually dined with two middle-aged men, a Mr Hopwood, who was an official of the Union Castle Line, and a Wing Commander Bray. Although polite and friendly to her companions, dining and dancing with them, for example, no doubt the young woman would have welcomed more congenial companionship – or even a little shipboard flirtation. But if she sought romance, it would have to come from a member of the crew, rather than from among her fellow passengers.

Just two days out from the Cape and it was noted that Miss Gibson was spending a good deal of time talking animatedly to the deck steward, Camb. He must have exuded male confidence. He remembered fondly those pleasure cruises before the war, when bored women took long sea cruises for the sole purpose of having a quick fling. The crews of most liners regarded this as being one of the 'perks' of the job.

For his part, Camb saw in Gay Gibson a young woman of some beauty, with alabaster skin and large almond-shaped eyes which were very expressive; her face was framed with long dark hair. Her acting experience had given her a superficial air of sophistication and self-assurance which she was far from feeling. Her background – unlike her complexion – was not untarnished.

She must have been worried to distraction by her unwanted pregnancy, which was aggravated by medical problems regarding respiration, causing her attacks similar to asthma. All these ingredients were to play a significant role in the tragedy which unfolded aboard that ship.

The developing relationship between Miss Gibson

and the steward did not go unnoticed in the small, closed universe of a ship at sea. The senior man on night watch saw them together, and even overheard fragments of their conversation. Officially, the crew members were strictly forbidden to form personal relationships with passengers, and the main difficulty standing in the way of the oversexed Camb's attempts to seduce Miss Gibson lay in the fact that as a deck steward he had no right to be in the cabins. If found in those quarters, he would be dismissed the ship, his papers being marked in such a way that he would never again find a job at sea.

Camb knew all this. It was a straight choice between his career and his passion. He chose passion. It was to cost him not only his job, but almost his life . . .

The night of 17 October 1947 was to be the last in the life of Gay Gibson. That night she dined as usual with Mr Hopwood and Wing Commander Bray. She danced for a short time and then, since it was a hot night, left to go to her cabin on B Deck to get her swimsuit, intending to have a dip in the ship's swimming pool. However, she returned half an hour later, saying she couldn't find her costume.

But during this half-hour time gap she had been seen by the senior night-watchman talking to Camb. He heard Camb say to her: 'I say, I have a bone to pick with you, and a big one at that.' It was Camb's job to prepare tea for the passengers, the trays being taken to the cabins by a stewardess. Camb was heard asking Miss Gibson if she would like him to prepare her a supper tray or bring her some lemonade. He added words to the effect that he had a good mind to bring her a drink down and join her. Her reply was: 'Please yourself. It's up to you.'

At 12.40 a.m. on 18 October, Miss Gibson was escorted to her cabin by Mr Hopwood. But twenty minutes later the boatswain's mate saw her leaning over the rail at the after end of the promenade deck, smoking a cigarette and seeking fresh air in the hot and humid night. The mate thought she looked a pretty picture in her long black evening gown and silver dancing slippers. However, since he was in charge of a party swabbing the deck, he had to ask her to move for fear she would get her feet wet. The mate was thus to become a vital witness, because Miss Gibson was never seen again after 1 a.m. – alive or dead – except by her killer.

At 2.58 a.m. on that same early morning the bell push in cabin No. 126 was pressed, ringing in the night-watchman's galley, and senior night-watchman Murray despatched his assistant, Steer, to find out what was wanted. Steer followed the lights in the passage until he reached Cabin 126. He could see light coming through the fanlight above the door, and saw to his surprise that both red and green lights were shining, indicating that both bell pushes had been pressed, for both the steward and stewardess, suggesting an emergency. Had just one bell push been pressed, the signal would have gone to the other night-watchman.

It had taken Steer under a minute to reach the cabin. He heard no sound from within the cabin and got no reply to his knocking. He tried the door handle and found it unlocked, and pushed open the door a couple of inches before it was slammed firmly in his face. But in that instant and through the gap he had seen and recognized the face of Camb, who shouted: 'All right.'

Steer went back to the galley to report having seen Camb in the cabin. Both men, Murray and Steer, then went to Cabin 126, but found the lights out, including the bell push indicators. The men went away, but reported the occurrence to the officer on the bridge, saying merely that they had seen a man in Miss Gibson's cabin. They did not mention Camb's name, for fear of getting a colleague into trouble. The officer then said there was nothing he could do about it, it was not for him to interfere with the passenger's morals.

It was four hours later, at 7.30 a.m., when Miss Field,

the stewardess, knocked on the door of Cabin 126 to ask if breakfast was required. There was no reply. The cabin door was unlocked and Miss Gibson was missing. Miss Field did not immediately suspect foul play, thinking Miss Gibson might have gone to the bathroom. She noted that her evening dress was hanging in its usual place, although her dressing gown and black pyjamas were missing. She also noted that the bedding was disarranged, with some stains to the sheets and pillow. The porthole was wide open . . .

It was only later, when Miss Field asked the bedroom steward if Miss Gibson had had a bath and was told 'No' that she became alarmed and reported her missing. When Miss Gibson failed to respond to the captain's broadcast throughout the ship, he reversed course and travelled back over his own wake for over an hour, with lookouts seeking a body in the water. It was futile, as he well knew. If she had not drowned immediately, the sharks would have got her. Reluctantly, at 11.40 a.m., the captain resumed his original course.

Convinced that Miss Gibson had vanished through that open porthole, the captain now set about questioning the crew, and Steer told him about having seen Camb in the missing girl's cabin. Camb was sent for, and, not realizing he had been recognized, immediately answered questions with a pack of lies, to protect himself and his job. In answer to questions, he denied having been anywhere near the passengers' cabins, and said he had retired to bed at 12.45 a.m.

Captain Patey did not tell Camb he had been seen in the cabin, but suggested to him that he had been in the vicinity of Cabin 126 at 3 a.m. Camb flatly denied this. Camb's cabinmate, William Pott, told the captain that Camb had come on duty that morning wearing steward's full dress – a long-sleeved jacket – which was unusual, given that Camb had routine cleaning duties.

Suspecting that Camb had worn the jacket to hide marks on his arms, the captain ordered the ship's doctor to examine the man. Dr Griffiths found scratches to Camb's back and right wrist, scratches which could well have been caused by a woman's sharp fingernails . . .

Camb, although not under arrest, was relieved of his duties for the rest of the voyage. Knowing he was a prime suspect for murder, Camb wrote two notes to his captain. In the first he denied having been anywhere near Cabin 126. In the second he attempted to explain his scratches by blaming them on rough towels and catching himself with his own nails.

Cabin 126 had been sealed with a special padlock, and following the disappearance of Miss Gibson, many wild rumours circulated. One was to the effect that a shark had been caught off the African coast, and when slit open its stomach was found to contain a woman's painted fingernail.

The liner steamed into Southampton on the morning of 25 October, and at 1.25 a.m. Detective Sergeant Quinlan of Southampton Borough Police boarded the ship to begin his inquiries. After talking to passengers and crew members, at 5.25 a.m. he interviewed Camb, who again denied having been near Miss Gibson's cabin. Told that he had been *seen* there, Camb replied weakly: 'That puts me in a tight spot.'

Questioned later by Detective Sergeant (Acting Inspector) Gibbons, Camb finally admitted that he had been down to the cabin – but only to ask Miss Gibson if she wanted a drink. She had been searching for a swimming costume – confirmed by her friend Mr Hopwood. Gibbons then offered Camb a remarkable escape clause. He told him: 'You are being given an opportunity to make any explanation . . . That explanation, so far, has been a categorical denial that you know anything about the death of Miss Gibbons. You may find that such a complete denial will be difficult to explain later . . .'

Camb asked: 'Does that mean I murdered her and that I shall be charged with murder?'

Mr Gibbons replied: 'We have to give particular care to any explanation you may put forward. You may be able to give a reasonable explanation for the cause of her death and disappearance.'

Camb then said: 'You mean that Miss Gibson might have died from some other cause, other than being murdered? She might have had a heart attack or something?'

In this last remark may lie the whole clue to this case. The prosecution asserted that Camb was being invited to invent a heart attack; the defence maintained that this was nothing but the truth. The detective had explained to the worried Camb how a woman had come to die suddenly in his arms, and in a flash he saw the truth of the explanation and was relieved. It would be left to a jury to decide the issue of Camb's guilt or innocence.

Camb had made a written statement admitting having pushed the body of Gay Gibson through the porthole of her cabin. He had also made verbal remarks about his many affairs with female passengers. In all he had been remarkably indiscreet for a murderer . . .

The trial of James Camb for the murder of Gay Gibson took place in a temporary assize court built in the Great Hall of Winchester Castle and presided over by King Arthur's Round Table. Plywood partitions had been erected to form the court, the prisoner having to mount five steps to reach a narrow rail-guarded walk of some six feet to the dock. Once there, Camb found himself perched high above the court, virtually isolated as if in the crow's-nest of a ship.

The proceedings began on Thursday, 18 March 1948, before Mr Justice Hilbery. The prosecution was led by Mr G. D. (Khaki) Roberts, KC, while the defence lay in the hands of Mr J. D. Casswell, KC. Both men were among the leading barristers of their time.

The defence had not been idle in the months which had elapsed since the arrest of Camb. Camb's solicitor,

Mr Geoffrey Wells, had been impressed with Camb's knowledge of the dead girl's private life. These were details which could only have come from the girl herself. Just four days out at sea and she had told Camb that she was three months pregnant – or so Camb had said to Miss Field, the stewardess. When he asked her why she did not marry the man responsible, she had replied that the man – 'Charlie' – was married, but she was 'crazy' about him. She had also told Camb that she had gone to South Africa for her health, as she suffered from asthma.

Mr Wells now had inquiries instituted in South Africa, and as a result discovered that Miss Gibson had travelled out there in an emigrant ship but had returned first-class, her fare having been paid by a Mr Charles Sventonski, from whom she had received a total of £500. He was a wealthy businessman who said he was willing to back Gay's career as a business proposition, and he gave her a letter of introduction to the Abbey Theatre, Dublin.

From the stewardess it was learned that a female contraceptive had been found in Miss Gibson's cabin in an unlocked suitcase. Fellow members of the repertory theatre, in which Miss Gibson had played the leading lady, were interviewed and made revealing statements. All had known of her pregnancy – she had tried to borrow money from them to pay for an English doctor. She often had breathing difficulties, and had once fainted with saliva coming from her mouth. In addition, she often complained of a shooting pain in her left arm. These were possible symptoms of heart or lung disease. Three members of the cast were brought over to England to give evidence for the defence.

If the prosecution wished to present Miss Gibson as a nice girl of impeccable character, then the defence had evidence which painted a very different story. It suggested a tale of a highly sexed ship's steward getting together with a girl of somewhat dubious morals for a night of mutually agreed fun of a sexual nature. Fun which had gone tragically wrong . . .

Sure enough, the prosecution began with a character attack against Camb. When first questioned by Detective Sergeant Quinlan, Camb had been asked if he ever had relations with passengers. Somewhat unwisely, perhaps, Camb had boasted of many sordid little affairs with unattached female passengers, adding: 'Some of them like us better than the other passengers. I have been with them several times on other trips.' He had added: 'Of course, if I was found out, I would get the sack.' This suggested a possible motive: murder to save his job. The ship's master confirmed that had Camb been found in a passenger's cabin, his book would have been endorsed and he would have found it difficult to get another job at sea. The jury were not allowed to know about Camb's assaults on other women, since it would have been prejudicial.

It was the Crown's case that James Camb had strangled Miss Gibson on the morning of 18 October 1947, afterwards throwing her body out into the shark-infested sea through the porthole of her cabin, in order to conceal evidence of his crime, which was that he had raped, or had attempted to rape, the girl, she had resisted and raised the alarm, and Camb had killed her to preserve his job and to prevent her from giving evidence against him.

The prosecution admitted that it was purely a case of circumstantial evidence, since there was no body to prove cause of death, but insisted that the medical evidence to be presented would confirm beyond doubt that Miss Gibson had been strangled. The prosecution opened its case by asking the jury: 'Is Eileen Gibson dead?'

Further evidence of a controversial nature was offered. Camb was alleged to have said, when alone with a detective constable: 'She struggled. I had my arms around her neck, and when I was trying to pull them away she scratched me. I panicked and threw her out of the porthole. It was a hell of a splash when she hit the water. I cannot understand why the officer of the watch did not hear something.'

It was suggested that the constable was lying. It would have been an incredibly stupid thing for Camb to have said, knowing he was facing a murder charge. He would have known that any splash could not possibly have been heard above the noise of the machinery in the dummy funnel and the backlash from the bow wave. It was subsequently established that the constable had 'left the force before the trial to better himself, but was still unemployed'.

Also offered into evidence was Camb's own apparently self-incriminating statement, which did not endear him to the jury. A man who was so supremely selfish that he put his job before the life of a young girl, 'concluding she was dead' but not seeking medical aid to make sure, before thrusting her body out of the porthole. Camb may well have been innocent, but that statement sealed his fate. No jury could have forgiven so brutal and callous an action. Camb himself admitted under cross-examination that his conduct had been 'beastly'.

Camb's statement read:

> I went to Miss Gibson's cabin at about eleven o'clock, and during the course of conversation with her I made an appointment to meet her that night. I knocked at the door after I had finished work at about one o'clock, but there was no answer. I opened the door of her cabin and found it empty. I then went forward to the well deck where I sat for about half an hour smoking. I then returned to Miss Gibson's cabin at about two o'clock and found her there. After a short conversation I got into bed with her consent. Intimacy took place. Whilst in the act of sexual intercourse she clutched me, foaming at the mouth. I immediately ceased the act, but she was very still; I felt for her heart beats, but could not find any. She was at that time very still, and I cannot offer any

explanation as to how the bells came to be rung, as I most definitely did not touch them myself. Thinking she had fainted, I tried artificial respiration on her. Whilst doing this the night-watchman knocked at the door and attempted to open it. I shut the door again, saying it was all right. Then I panicked, as I thought he had gone to the bridge to report to the officer of the watch, and I did not want to be found in such a compromising position. After a few minutes I could not find any signs of life. After a struggle with the limp body – by the way, she was still wearing her dressing gown – I managed to lift her to the porthole and push her through. I am fairly certain that at the time she was dead, but I was terribly frightened. I then went forward and turned in. The time would be about 3.30 a.m.

After adding that he was glad he had got the matter off his mind, Camb said: 'What will happen about this? My wife must not know about this. If she does, I will do away with myself.'

Mr Roberts began his opening address by saying: 'Members of the jury, to some extent this is an unusual case. There is no body here, no *corpus delecti*, as the lawyers say. It is unusual, but it is by no means unprecedented . . .'

In the courtroom a mock cabin had been built, with the bed from Cabin 126, a porthole of the same size as those of the *Durban Castle* mounted in a wooden frame, a bell push at the head of the bed, and a small chest. Other exhibits included plans of the cabin and cabin deck, and photographs, as well as the bedding from Cabin 126.

The Crown now began calling its witnesses to prove from circumstantial evidence alone that Camb had murdered the missing girl by strangulation. Members of the ship's crew testified as to what they knew. The night-watchman had seen Camb in Cabin 126, following the ringing of the alarm bell from that cabin. Others had seen Camb and the girl together. The stewardess had found the empty cabin, with its bed linen soiled. Camb had lied to the captain. The ship's doctor had found scratch marks on his person. Fibres from the dead girl's dressing gown had been found on the inside edge and outside edge of the porthole, and Camb's palm print had been found on the door of Cabin 126.

The dead girl's mother testified, stating firmly: 'I am proud to be her mother. She was the finest type of English womanhood, physically, mentally and morally.'

The doctor's findings were the most important evidence against Camb. He testified that he had found three main groups of injuries on Camb. There were recent scratches over the back of the right shoulder, old scratches over the left collar bone and, most significant of all, twelve deep scratches lying horizontally across Camb's right lower arm, probably caused by fingernails digging into the flesh in a 'dragging' motion.

The Crown said the scratches were caused by Miss Gibson fighting for her life and attempting to pull away the choking hands from her throat. The defence maintained the scratches were caused by Miss Gibson grasping Camb's arm tightly while having a fit which killed her.

The medical evidence was crucial. Dr Montgomery, a senior scientific officer at the Metropolitan Laboratory at Hendon, testified that he had examined the bedding from Cabin 126. On the top sheet he found saliva and two small spots of blood of Group O. Camb was Group A. In other words, the dead girl had bled before death, as happens in cases of strangulation when blood may issue from the mouth or nose.

Dr (later Professor) Donald Teare was a noted pathologist, and was the chief medical witness for the prosecution. He was later to enjoy fame as one of the 'Three Musketeers' of pathology, the other two being Francis Camps and Keith Simpson. Between them they were involved in most of the big post-war murder trials. Teare later became involved in the cases of the 'Cleft-Chin Murder', (taxi-driver killing) Podola (the murder of DS Purdy), and Timothy Evans.

Asked to describe the signs he would expect to find in a case of strangulation, Dr Teare described a slight haemorrhage from the lungs or upper air passages due to pressure on the neck – thus accounting for the blood marks on the sheet. Alternatively, the blood might have come from the victim when she scratched herself in attempting to relieve the pressure on her throat. Although he would make no comment about the scratches found on Camb, he did emphasize the urine stains found on the sheet, stressing that victims of strangulation voided themselves at the time of death.

Under cross-examination, Dr Teare conceded that the signs of muddiness visible in Miss Gibson's fingernails, and testified to by her friend Mr Hopwood, could indicate some sort of circulatory problem or heart disease.

The defence rebutted all the medical evidence with its own witnesses. The three members of the cast testified. All said Miss Gibson suffered from asthma attacks and occasionally collapsed. Mike Abel said she often behaved in a hysterical manner and her breathing was laboured. She also complained of a shooting pain in her arm which went right down to her fingertips. She had told him she was pregnant and tried to borrow £200 to get to England. Henry Gilbert testified that Gay had been highly strung and tended to drink too much. She had told him: 'I cannot love like other people' and 'I am not like other girls'. He assumed she meant that her breathing problems made normal intercourse impossible. Dr Ina Schoub, wife of Henry Gilbert, testified that Gay had discussed sex intimately with her and had talked about her pregnancy. Gay had told fellow cast members that her mother and father were dead, having been killed in the war. Since this was patently untrue, it suggested that she was simply a neurotic girl who told romantic and foolish lies about herself. Dr Schoub said of Gay: 'She was a nice girl, a charming girl.' The prosecutor said in his closing speech: 'Let that be her epitaph.'

Mr Casswell began the defence by maligning the character of the dead girl – as he had to – pointing out that she was not averse to receiving early morning visits from a presentable young man, even when she was naked. And she had a history of medical problems which indicated that the girl could have died in exactly the way described by Camb. Indeed, it was remarkable that Camb's account was so close to what might have been *expected* to happen in the circumstances.

The most important defence witness was Camb himself. He described the growing relationship between Gay and himself. He explained the remark 'I have a bone to pick with you' by reference to a special meal tray he had prepared for her which she had not collected. He then described the fatal night in question.

He went to Miss Gibson's cabin soon after 2 a.m. She was wearing nothing but a quilted yellow dressing gown. There were no black pyjamas anywhere in the cabin; Camb was adamant. Camb got on the bed beside the girl. She unzipped herself, revealing herself to be naked. They began to make love – and then Gay suddenly went stiff and unconscious, gripping his arm and scratching him. In his own words: 'I immediately got off the bed. She was completely relaxed, as though she was in a dead faint. One eye was slightly open. There was a faint line of bubbles which I assumed to be froth, just on the edge of her lips.'

Camb claimed that he tried to revive her with artificial respiration, but finally realized she was dead, and panicked. He accidentally pressed the bell pushes with his thigh in his panic and, with his whole career in jeopardy, set about destroying any evidence against him. By pushing the body out of the porthole, he had hoped everyone would assume she had fallen overboard.

Mr Roberts began his cross-examination with the question: 'Would you describe yourself as a truthful man?'

It was an ironic question, given Camb's admitted lies. But Camb replied: 'I think so, sir.'

Roberts hammered home the point that if Camb's story was true, then he had destroyed his own positive evidence, since a post-mortem would have proved whether the girl had died from natural causes or not, and he would have been completely exonerated. (The judge was to stress the same point in his summing-up.)

Mr Roberts went on: 'The body, as you agree, is conclusive evidence as to the cause of death, and your first instinct is to destroy it. It is a curious instinct for an innocent man, is it not?'

Camb: 'I think it was an automatic instinct. I was being selfish at the time and thinking more about my job.'

'You sought no medical attention for this girl?'

'No, sir.'

Re-examined by Mr Casswell, Camb was asked: 'Are you proud of what you did that night?'

Camb replied: 'I am not, sir. I am ashamed . . . my conduct was beastly.'

Camb stood up to a gruelling cross-examination well, appearing calm and self-assured at all times. So calm that Mr Roberts was to ask the jury: 'Camb says he threw her through the porthole in a panic. Did he panic? Panic! Do you think he is the sort of man to panic? Did you see any sign of panic at all? Did you see any lack of poise, or composure or full control of the thinking faculties?'

For the defence, Professor Webster, a Home Office pathologist, testified that the evidence was consistent with Camb's story. He gave three instances in his experience of death during sexual intercourse by a rupture in the brain. In his opinion, Gay Gibson had died from a heart disease associated with asthma. He concluded that the probability of death from natural causes was greater than from strangulation. Dr Teare put it the other way round, but conceded the possibility of heart disease.

On any fair balancing of evidence, Camb should have been acquitted, but he had destroyed his own case by his statement and by his calm demeanour in the witness box. At the end of the four-day trial the judge summed up for four hours in so biased a way against Camb that Mr Casswell complained bitterly to him, reminding him of the many factors in favour of the defendant which he had neglected to mention. Mr Justice Hilbery said stonily: 'I have not attempted to mention everything, and I am not bound to do so.'

In the course of his somewhat one-sided summing-up, the judge said: 'She was alive, Miss Field told us, when she was dressing the evening before for dinner; she was then a gay and happy young woman; yet by three o'clock in the morning she was dead and her body being stuffed, bundled ignominiously through a porthole – you may think to hide something. And the question is: "What?" '

The judge put some vital questions to the jury. How did Camb come by the scratches on his wrist? What happened to the black pyjamas? Who rang the bells in Cabin 126? Camb said he had not, leaving the inference that Miss Gibson had done so to summon help. Why did Camb throw the body overboard? He stressed that if, as Camb said, she had died from natural causes, the most obvious thing for him to have done would be to have slipped quietly away from her cabin, leaving her to be found the following morning. But if her throat bore marks of strangulation, then Camb *dared* not let her body be found . . .

After deliberating for just forty minutes, on 22 March 1948 the jury found Camb guilty. Asked if he had anything to say before sentence of death was passed, Camb replied: 'My Lord, at the opening of this case I pleaded not guilty, and I repeat that statement now.'

The case went to the Appeal Court, presided over by the Lord Chief Justice, Lord Goddard. While admitting that 'undoubtedly the learned Judge's summing-up was not favourable to the prisoner', Lord Goddard quoted precedents to the effect that the trial judge was entitled to give some assistance to the jury on questions of fact as well as law. The appeal was dismissed without the Crown even being called to answer the defence arguments. It is alleged that afterwards Mr Justice Humphreys, one of the judges who sat to hear the appeal, remarked: 'That man wasn't given a chance.' Yet in his *A Book of Trials* (1953) Travers Humphreys is adamant that Camb was rightly convicted. He describes the case as being 'yet another instance of convincing proof of the guilt of an accused person being afforded by circumstantial evidence'.

Mr Casswell believed firmly in Camb's innocence, and affirms that belief in his book *A Lance for Liberty*.

Although sentenced to hang, Camb was reprieved on 30 April 1948 because Parliament was debating the 'no hanging' clause of the Criminal Justice Bill. He served a life sentence, and was released from prison in September 1959.

There remains the mystery of the black pyjamas. Camb was adamant that Gay Gibson was not wearing them. There appears to be no reason why Camb should have lied about such a trivial point, and yet they were never found. What had happened to them? Rumour had it that they were in the possession of a distinguished male fellow passenger, Gay having left them in his cabin. The man was alleged to have said that he would come forward if there was any danger of Camb being hanged. There was indeed a period of time – from 1 a.m. to 2 a.m. – which remained unaccounted for and in which Gay could well have visited another cabin.

Much had been made of the black pyjamas in cross-examination, the prosecution contending that Gay had been wearing them and was therefore not inviting sexual intercourse. Camb insisted that no black pyjamas were in evidence, and he was the only person who knew the full truth of Gay Gibson's last moments. Since he died some years ago, any knowledge of the black pyjamas died with him.

It remains a rare case. On balance, the legal profession approves of the conviction, while the medical profession agree that Camb was probably innocent.

5
MICHIAL ONUFREJCZYK: GALLANT SOLDIER TURNED KILLER.

Onufrejczyk – pronounced 'Ono-free-shic' – was born in in Poland. That unhappy country had the misfortune to become a victim of war twice this century, and Michial Onufrejczyk served in them both, as a soldier in the Polish Army. In the First World War he was wounded twice and decorated; in the Second World War he won nine medals for gallantry, serving with the Free Polish Army, which was stationed in Britain but saw action in many theatres of war, including the battle for Monte Cassino in Italy.

The end of the war saw him discharged in England as a warrant officer, and so like many Poles who fought for Britain during the war, he settled in this country. He joined the Polish Resettlement Corps in Wales, an organization dedicated to helping Poles to find homes and occupations, even to the extent of making them generous loans for this purpose.

Onufrejczyk decided to become a farmer, and bought a farm at Cwn Du in Carmarthenshire, South Wales. The farm was called Cefn Hendre, and it seemed a good buy to the Pole, who was given a loan from the Polish Army's reserve funds to make the purchase. However, it was a pity he never sounded out local farmers on the idea. They could have told him that hard work alone would never make the farm a paying proposition; the soil was poor and one man could not handle livestock alone.

Onufrejczyk moved into the farm in 1949 and bought some livestock. He lived alone, an erect military man who was quite self-sufficient. But he was no farmer and certainly no businessman. The farm drifted into bankruptcy, reaching the point when Onufrejczyk, unable to meet his bills, had to search for desperate solutions to his cash problem.

He turned to an old army comrade, Stanislaw Sykut, who was working as a male nurse in Shropshire. Sykut, at fifty-seven, was a year younger than Onufrejczyk, but not as physically fit. However, he was impressed with his companion's talk of how the farm could prove to be a gold mine, and parted with £600 to buy a half-share in the farm, moving in sometime in March 1953.

Relations between the two men quickly deteriorated. The powerfully built Onufrejczyk became impatient with his companion's inability to pick up the rudiments of farming quickly, and the money Sykut had brought into the business quickly evaporated, leaving them no better off financially. Onufrejczyk, always a quick-tempered and volatile man, began physically abusing his partner, once knocking him about so badly that Sykut went to the local police station on 18 May 1953 to register a complaint.

That brought Sergeant Phillips to the farm to make inquiries. He knew of the two men, since they were listed in the aliens register at the police station. He asked the bearded Onufrejczyk why he had been hitting his partner. He, alarmed at the sight of an official uniform, tried to placate the officer by saying: 'Partner no work. But me, I no hit partner again. Now we both understand good, I tell you.'

The sergeant went away, having listed the details in his note-book and administered a caution. However, relations between the two Poles remained poor and charged with friction. Just a month after the start of the partnership – on 10 April 1953 – Onufrejczyk gave Sykut six months' notice of his intention to dissolve it.

However, Sykut remained on the farm after the expiration of this notice – which fell due on 14 November – because Onufrejczyk could not afford to buy out his half-share. Certainly Sykut was seen about the farm as late as December. In fact, Sykut was last seen alive by a local blacksmith on 14 December, to be precise.

Sergeant Phillips, who had helped find the bodies of John and Phoebe Harries – who had been murdered by their nephew and buried on their Carmarthenshire farm – just a month before, had occasion to visit Cefn Hendre again on 30 December, to make a routine check on aliens – such checks were routine and were being made all over Britain. He found Sykut missing.

Asked to explain the whereabouts of his partner, the fifty-nine-year-old Onufrejczyk claimed that his partner had left the farm on the morning of 18 December without notice. He had no idea where he had gone. Pressed for details, Onufrejczyk said that a large black car had arrived with three strange Poles in it and had taken Sykut away. He thought the car was from the Polish Embassy.

Sergeant Phillips was not satisfied. He asked to look round the farmhouse, and noted articles belonging to Sykut, including his shaving gear. He was especially interested in extensive bloodstains on one wall. He talked to Onufrejczyk again, who this time said that he thought his partner had decided to return to Poland, because he had sold him his half-share of the farm for £450 in cash and a credit note for £150. He produced a document which he claimed had been signed by Sykut and witnessed by the three mystery Poles. It was effectively a bill of sale.

The notion that a man would willingly return to life behind the Iron Curtain seemed ludicrous to Sergeant Phillips, who lost no time in alerting his superior, Inspector Fred Fox, about his suspicions. He suspected murder from the start.

Leaving Onufrejczyk alone on the farm for the time

being, the police began checking his story. They discovered that Sykut had not left the country to return to Poland – at least, not by any airline flight or ship. And he had not used his passport at any point of exit. He had not said goodbye to any of his friends, and had left £450 in his Post Office savings account. And since 14 December, uncollected mail had been gathering at the local post office.

The highly sceptical police officers called on Onufrejczyk again, to ask more searching questions. They looked at the document which allegedly passed Sykut's half-share over, and kept it to examine the signature for possible forgery. Having checked bank records and discovered the amount of Onufrejczyk's indebtedness, they asked him where he had got the £450 from to pay off his partner. He claimed he had been loaned this sum by a Mrs Pokora, who lived in London.

The police now discovered that Onufrejczyk had been to see the local blacksmith in an attempt to persuade him to say that he had seen Sykut on the seventeenth. The blacksmith refused; it had been the fourteenth. The police also had Scotland Yard detectives question Mrs Pokora. She denied ever having lent any money to Onufrejczyk, but had an interesting story to tell. She said he had visited her at her home on 21 December and had asked her to *pretend* to loan him the money by sending him two registered packets to the local post office. She had refused. As for the document transferring ownership of the farm to Onufrejczyk, *she* had written it at his dictation.

The Pole was visited once again by the police, who confronted him with his lies. They also took the opportunity to thoroughly search the farm, having obtained a warrant for this purpose. Evidence of severe bloodstaining suggested that Sykut had been killed in the farmhouse – Onufrejczyk said the blood had come from rabbits he had killed and skinned. He could not explain why Sykut had left so many of his personal belongings behind, including his shaving brush and razor.

He now came up with a fresh set of lies. He said he had met one of the three mystery Poles – Jablonski by name – at Paddington on 21 December and had been given written instructions from Sykut regarding the drawing-up of the document, which he then had Mrs Pokora do. But a Mrs Nowak, whom the police had traced, said that she had visited the farm on 20 December, and Onufrejczyk had at that time talked of his plans to buy Sykut out. The whole fabric of his lies was being destroyed.

He had told the police that the transaction had been completed on the night of 18 December, yet here he was two days later still contemplating buying his partner out. Prosecuting counsel was to tell the jury at his trial: 'If you believe the evidence of Mrs Nowak, then the whole story of the Friday night visit by the three men goes absolutely and utterly by the board; it is simply untenable.'

Onufrejczyk had been asked to account for his partner's movements prior to his disappearance. He said Sykut had visited a doctor on 18 December – but no doctor could be found who had treated the man. He also claimed that Sykut had visited the blacksmith to have a horse shod on 17 December; the blacksmith swore it was 14 December. In other words, he was making a determined effort to show that Sykut had been alive *after* the fourteenth – which suggested to the police that he had been dead by that date.

The matter was now considered to be very serious by the local police, who had caused an area of forty miles around the farm to be searched for any sign of Sykut's secret burial place, without result. The Chief Constable of Carmarthenshire now took the step of calling in Scotland Yard's fabled murder squad.

Detective Superintendent Jamieson visited Onufrejczyk at his farm, leaving him in no doubt that he was dissatisfied with his story. Point by point the officer outlined the discrepancies in his story. He claimed blood on the kitchen wall came from a rabbit, and from a time when Sykut had cut his finger, yet it was known he had assaulted Sykut, and the bloodstains proved to be of human origin. Mrs Pokora had denied lending him any money. Sykut had not been seen alive after 14 December, and the officer believed that he was dead, the victim of murder.

Onufrejczyk shook his head stubbornly, denying everything and saying: 'I do not wish to talk to you. I have no more to say. You can hang me if you like.'

During the next few months evidence was painstakingly collected, but lacking a body – that final proof of murder – the case was discussed with the Director of Public Prosecutions. For almost three hundred years in English criminal history there had been no conviction for murder without either identification of the body or part of the body, or at least a confession from the accused indicating that the victim was dead – as with Davidson in 1934.

The case of James Camb in 1947 was a precedent of sorts, although the evidence had been strong and Camb had confessed to pushing the body of his victim out of a porthole.

However, legal advice was given to the effect that circumstantial evidence alone could prove guilt, if strong enough; a recent judgement in the New Zealand Court of Appeal was cited supporting this contention.

That judgement, in *Rex v. Horry*, 1952, read:

> In the trial of a person charged with murder the fact of death is provable by circumstantial evidence, notwithstanding that neither the body nor any trace of the body has been found, and the accused has made no confession to any participation in the crime. Before he can be convicted the fact of death must be proved by such circumstances as to render the commission of the crime morally certain and leave no ground for reasonable doubt. The circumstantial evidence should be so cogent and compelling as to convince a jury that upon no rational hypothesis other than murder can the fact be accounted for.

In view of the facts in the case, the known bad blood between Onufrejczyk and his partner, the lies he had told the police, and the fact that Sykut was missing and could not be accounted for, the DPP was satisfied that there was enough circumstantial evidence to try the Pole for the murder of his partner, the obvious motive being greed. He had killed to gain sole control of the farm; that much was certain. But would a jury of Welshmen convict in a case where foreigners were concerned? Foreigners who were likely to do strange things – including returning to their native land – and where no body could be produced to prove murder? The accused – a man with a distinguished war record, who had to prove nothing – was likely to say in court: 'He is not dead.' The burden of proving that Sykut was indeed dead lay on the Crown, and it was no easy burden.

Accordingly, almost a year later, on 19 August 1954, Onufrejczyk was arrested and charged with the murder of Sykut. On 14 September he appeared before the magistrates in Llandeilo for a five-week hearing, at the end of which they decided there was a case to answer and committed him to Swansea Assizes for trial.

In November 1954 the trial began before Mr Justice Oliver, and was to create a legal precedent. It was also to last an astonishing twelve days, the longest in recent history at that time. This was mainly because the accused could speak little English, and all the court proceedings had to be translated for him by a court interpreter.

In his opening speech for the prosecution, Mr Edmund Davies, QC, outlined the facts of the case, and then told the all-male jury: 'We say the accused was driven by desperation by the motive which since history began has driven men to commit murder – he did it for sheer greed.'

Mr Davies went on: 'For a few months during 1953 there lived in a lonely farm in the heart of rural Carmarthenshire two men. They were Poles. One of them had been there since 1949; the other arrived only in March last year. No one else lived with them in that farm . . .

'Their life together was a bitter one, for soon, very soon, there arose quarrels between them and physical assaults by one man upon the other, causing the other man to seek police protection. Their life together was a short one, for after only eight months the man who arrived in March disappeared – disappeared as completely as though the earth had swallowed him up.

'The remarkably remorseless procession of facts – not conjectures or guesses – but *facts*, and not one fact or a dozen facts but hundreds of facts, point inevitably to one conclusion only – that he was murdered by the man in the dock. No one saw him do it, and the Crown is unable to call an eyewitness who can tell you at what hour he did it, or what weapons he employed to accomplish his murderous design.

'The prosecution have to prove that Sykut is dead and that he met his death at the hands of Onufrejczyk in circumstances amounting to murder. No body has been discovered, but it is not the law that a charge of murder cannot be brought home unless either the body of the victim has been found or there is a confession of guilt. If that was the position, that would be to grant a charter of protection to any murderer who is cunning enough to see to it that his victim's body is disposed of without trace. This matter has been the subject of a number of decisions recently. There was one in New Zealand in 1952, and in Ireland in June this year. In both these cases English law applied.'

The jury of hard-headed Welshmen sat and listened to the rich oratory of the prosecutor, and they must have been thinking: Fine talk – but where is the *evidence*?

Mr Davies sketched in the background to the case. A week after Sykut was last seen alive – by the village blacksmith – Onufrejczyk went to London, where he attempted to persuade various people to forge Sykut's signature on several documents. At this point he was in severe financial difficulties, with a mortgage of £1,600 and debts of £334. He had approached banks for loans, without success.

He had taken Sykut into partnership on 10 April 1953 – principally for the money he could bring into the business. Sykut was a physically frail man who was to become terrified of the robust and aggressive Onufrejczyk, who complained that he was too weak to work the farm. Within days he was knocking him about, and within a month had given him six months' notice of his intention to dissolve the partnership. But Onufrejczyk's solicitor told him that unless he bought out Sykut's share of the farm, for which he had paid a total of £730, the farm would have to be put up for auction. Onufrejczyk stood to lose everything. He could not buy Sykut out – he had no money – and his only solution was to murder him.

The court would hear that in August Onufrejczyk had told a friend: 'I cannot stand it any longer. I shall take an axe and I will finish everything.' This was evidence of premeditation. During October he went to Llandeilo and left two steel cases, which he never reclaimed, with a fellow Pole. When opened by the police later, they were found to contain new suits of clothing and underlinen, presumably Sykut's.

There was no doubt that Onufrejczyk had pursued a policy of violence and intimidation, with the intention of driving Sykut out of the farm. But the weaker man clung on tenaciously. On 21 and 22 December, Onufrejczyk visited London and had Sykut's signature forged on several documents, including that bill of sale and blank cheques. He also sent Mrs Pokora a letter thanking her for sending him £450 through the post, a letter which mystified her, since she had never sent him a penny.

Onufrejczyk later visited her at her house in London and told her that Sykut was returning to Poland. Mrs Pokora did not believe this tale. Bluntly, she accused him of having murdered his partner. He did not refute this allegation. Instead, he went very pale and nervous. Mrs Pokora would later say that the prisoner started to sob, and then came out with a 'cloak-and-dagger story' of how Sykut had been abducted by officials from the Polish Embassy. After the police called at the farm on 30 December, the alarmed Onufrejczyk wrote to Mrs Pokora begging her to tell anyone who inquired that she had loaned him the money to buy out Sykut.

All this was evidence of suspicious behaviour, indicative of guilty knowledge. Now Mr Davies turned to the physical evidence. Despite a search of a forty-mile area around the farm, no trace of Sykut or his remains had been found. But inside the farmhouse police had found evidence of his life – and death. There were bloodstains, thousands of them; some had even sprayed on to the ceiling.

'On the dresser was found the imprint of a bloodstained hand; on a plasterboard beside the fireplace were found 2,728 bloodstains. They were found to be human bloodstains.'

At the local post office, thirteen letters from Poland lay waiting for Sykut to pick up. He never did, because, Mr Davies alleged, he was dead. A handwriting expert testified that Sykut's signature had been forged on various documents.

The Crown had finished presenting its case, and now it was the turn of the defence. It called its first and only witness, Onufrejczyk himself, who went into the witness box to testify on his own behalf. His counsel asked him if he had indeed killed his partner, as the prosecution claimed. Onufrejczyk stroked his huge beard and said flatly: 'Sykut is alive.'

Asked to explain how he had come to tell lies to the police, Onufrejczyk said that he spoke poor English and had been misunderstood. Asked to explain how he had come by the money with which he claimed he had bought out Sykut's half of the farm, the prisoner admitted a little larceny.

He said he had smuggled the money into England in

1947, when he had returned from serving as a warrant officer in the Polish forces. Fearing the income tax authorities, he could not put the money into any bank. He had tried to get Mrs Pokora to pretend to have loaned him the money simply to hide his true financial position from the Inland Revenue. It was a clever, well-thought-out line of defence. But he had enjoyed over a year in which to think it up.

In cross-examination Mr Davies asked him: 'There was only one way you could stop Sykut from selling that farm by auction, wasn't there, by killing him?'

Defiantly, Onufrejczyk said: 'I never thought of such a thing. I did not regard an auction sale of the farm as spelling ruin for me.'

'No three men came to the farm on 18 December, did they?'

Onufrejczyk persisted in his story. 'They came. A big car, also.'

Onufrejczyk now claimed that the blood found in the kitchen of the farmhouse came from a time when Sykut had cut his hand on farm machinery, after analysis had found that they were human bloodstains and had not come from rabbits, as he had originally stated. But he refused to have his own blood tested to establish whether the bloodstains could have come from him.

In the absence of the jury, counsel for the defence, Mr Elwyn Jones, asked the judge if he thought it proper for him to tell the jury that he could find no case in English criminal history for the last three hundred years where there had been a conviction for murder without either a body or a confession. In effect, he was arguing that the recent New Zealand case and the Irish one were an attempt to change the law – or the custom of the law. The judge decided that he should make no such reference to the jury. The judge alone was responsible for interpreting the law to the jury.

In his final speech to the jury, Mr Davies said simply: 'If you are convinced that the accused lied hard to account for Sykut's disappearance, you are bound to ask why is he lying.'

In his closing speech to the jury, Mr Jones reminded them that they had to be sure that Sykut was dead, sure beyond a shadow of a doubt. Was it not possible that he had indeed returned to Poland? Or had even been kidnapped by Polish agents?

He added: 'We live in a curious world of revolution and counter-revolution, of espionage and counter-espionage, where even men in distinguished public positions disappear in the night, apparently without trace.' (He was no doubt referring to the defection of Burgess and Maclean to the Soviet Union on 25 May 1951. But they had at least granted press interviews upon their arrival in Moscow.)

Mr Jones concluded by asking the jury: 'Are you certain in your own minds that Sykut is dead? Are you certain that there is any evidence you can rely on that this man killed him? I submit to you that there is no room for such assertions.'

The judge summed up the case to the jury, asking them: 'Is it conceivable, do you think, that this man is alive? No one has heard or seen him since 14 December last year. It is indeed a grave step to find a murder proved where this is no body. But it is not the law that if a body be completely got rid of or concealed, no murderer can be convicted. If Sykut was killed by this man, then there is no question but that it was murder. If this was a crime, then it was one of the utmost premeditation, committed by a man who meant to get for nothing the half-share of the farm he was about to lose. He was a man who might be expected to take the most considerable trouble to escape retribution.'

It took the jury just under three hours to return with a verdict of guilty of murder. Telling them that he agreed with their verdict – 'I think it is a just one' – the judge then sentenced Onufrejczyk to death. His appeal was duly dismissed on 10 January, but on 23 January 1955 the Home Secretary, Mr Chuter Ede, granted a reprieve and commuted the death sentence to one of life imprisonment.

In reviewing all cases of a similar nature, there can be no doubt that there was a very real and almost superstitious reluctance to hang a convicted murderer when there was no body – for fear that the 'body' might reappear alive and well. And it is also possible that the Home Secretary had in mind the controversy over the recent case of Timothy Evans. One more 'innocent' man hanged might be one too many . . .

Later, the court was asked to presume Sykut dead so that his wife Janina and his daughter, living in Lublin, Poland, could inherit his estate. This was so ordered, but while the farm-stock was disposed of for £542, the joint partners had an overdraft of £1,525 with the bank. There was nothing to send to Poland.

Onufrejczyk served ten years in prison before being released. He settled near Bradford. But in 1966 he was killed in a road accident, taking with him the secret of what happened to the mortal remains of Stanislaw Sykut.

There is a footnote to this case. In November 1954, in a speech at the Mansion House which aroused controversy, Lord Chief Justice Goddard, who had presided over the Onufrejczyk appeal, suggested that juries in murder trials should be reduced to seven, and that a majority verdict should be accepted.

Sir Travers Humphreys retorted in a letter to *The Times*, on 10 November 1954:

> Abolish unanimity and you abolish the jury system. The 'verdict of you all' is part of the unwritten constitution of our country.

Now, of course, we *do* accept majority verdicts, and vetted juries. Despite Lord Goddard's remarks, the Onufrejczyk case had shown that with the old system, and even without a body, a jury could achieve a unanimous verdict. There seemed no reason to change a system that had worked so well for centuries.

6
JOE PEEL: THE JUDGE WHO PLOTTED MURDER

Beneath the spurious glamour of Florida – the 'Sunshine State' – there has always existed a sleazy and sinister dark underside. Even back in the fifties, before the advent of machine-gun-toting drug smugglers . . .

Just after 8.30 on the morning of 15 June 1955, two carpenters called at the beach house of Circuit Court Judge Curtis E. Chillingworth to repair a window frame. The house was situated on a dune overlooking the Atlantic, in the wealthy suburb of Manalapan. This meant it was located in the exclusive Palm Beach area, rather than the more common West Palm Beach, which was separated from its neighbour by Lake Worth. The difference was obvious to the eye. Palm Beach housed the huge mansions of millionaires, with luxury yachts moored at their private docks. It had just 2,500 permanent residents, whereas West Palm Beach had 60,000. Those figures said it all.

Judge Chillingworth, a tall, skinny man who wore spectacles, had been on the bench for thirty-four years and was the senior judge for the area. He had a town house, but used his beach house in the summer only, renting it out through the winter. The beach house boasted three bedrooms and a modern kitchen. At the rear, a flight of steps led down to the beach.

The two carpenters went to the rear of the house and found the building unlocked, with no one at home, although the judge's car stood in the two-car garage and he had arranged to meet the workmen that morning. His absence was most unusual, since he was a punctilious man, ascetic and almost humourless in his obsession with punctuality. The judge ran his private life, like his court, according to a rigid timetable.

The two workmen noticed that the rear porch light was broken and shards of glass lay on the decking. They went down to the beach, noting what appeared to be spots of blood on the steps. On the fine sand leading to the sea they saw many footprints, some going, others coming back, but even as they looked, the tide was washing away those prints.

Disturbed, the two men called the police, and Sheriff John Kirk responded to the call. He set up a temporary headquarters in a beach hut, while his deputies searched for clues. They found none. All that was established was that Judge Chillingworth and his wife Marjorie were missing. The judge had been due in court that morning, and his staff knew nothing of his whereabouts. The beds in the house had been slept in, and there was no sign of any struggle – even though the stains on the steps proved to be human blood. A long inquiry failed to locate any trace of the missing couple, and they were listed as missing, not dead. A reward of $100,000 for information was put on offer, but brought no response. Two years later the courts of Florida formally declared Judge Chillingworth and his wife to be legally dead, and there the case might have rested, a mysterious and insoluble disappearance.

The case broke slowly, as they have a habit of doing in real life. It took several years, in fact. The first hint came in an attempted murder case which happened two years later. Joseph Peel, a former municipal judge who heard only small cases and who had resigned after a couple of reprimands for disgraceful conduct, had begun practising law again and had hired as an assistant a young lawyer named Harold Gray. Judge Peel took out a $50,000 life insurance policy on Gray, with a double indemnity clause in case of death by violence. The insurance agent was James Yenzer, a man with a shady past who doubtless suspected what was planned. One evening Judge Peel invited Gray out for a drink. As they sat in a dim-lit bar, a man came out of the shadows and savagely attacked Gray with a club, only being driven off by other customers.

Gray was taken to hospital in a bad state, but he survived. Once again it fell to Sheriff John Kirk to investigate the affair, and when he discovered the existence of the insurance policy he arrested Yenzer and Judge Peel on charges of attempted murder. The actual attacker, Floyd Holzapfel, was arrested on a first-degree charge. However, at his subsequent trial Holzapfel convinced the jury that Gray had insulted his wife and he was acquitted. The charges against Judge Peel and Yenzer consequently had to be dropped.

But the case resulted in the police taking a closer look at Judge Peel. He had served two terms as the sole municipal judge for Palm Beach on a salary of just $3,000 a year. But he lived much more expensively than that; the handsome, wavy-haired young man drove an air-conditioned Cadillac, while his wife drove a Lincoln Continental. The source of his additional wealth was not hard to locate. He had used his influential position to demand bribes from racketeers engaged in illegal numbers betting and moonshine distilling, and from crooks operating protection rackets. He had protected these crooks from police raids by either alerting them when the police asked him to sign search warrants, or by drawing up the warrant defectively to ensure an acquittal on appeal.

Peel, just thirty-one, was born in West Palm Beach, and was a popular figure. He began practising law in 1949, and by 1953 was a minor judge who was to fall foul of both the law and a superior judge. On 6 July 1953 he had appeared before Circuit Judge Chillingworth on an ethics charge. He had represented both sides in a divorce case. Since the superior court judge was a stickler for the law, Peel was lucky to escape with a reprimand 'because of his youth and inexperience'. However, Judge Chillingworth let it be known that should Peel ever appear before him again on similar charges, he would be barred from practising law in Florida for life.

Shortly after this narrow escape, Peel asked State Attorney Phil O'Connell if he could give him some legal work. O'Connell did not think much of Peel, and even suspected his involvement in the rackets, but as an older man felt he had to encourage the young, and gave Peel an empty office in his building until he could establish a practice. The two men became friends, of a sort.

In 1954 Peel ran for re-election as municipal judge and won a second term. Now he grew ambitious, dreaming of perhaps becoming county solicitor, even State Senator, and ultimately even State Governor. To realize these ambitions Peel needed money, and perhaps the removal of possible rivals who stood in his way.

Whatever his shortcomings as a lawyer, Peel was not a stupid man. He had used his position to develop a network of shady contacts. For example, Floyd Holzapfel was a petty crook who once had dealings with Judge Peel. Peel took the man into his office and engaged him in jovial banter, letting him know that he knew all about him by using his nickname 'Lucky' and referring to his two convictions for armed robbery, his past history as a bookmaker, and the fact that he was now engaged in the sale of moonshine liquor. Such details did not bother the judge; they made Holzapfel 'useful' to know.

In a similar way he got close to a big black man named George David Lincoln – 'Bobby' to his friends – who owned two poolrooms, ran two taxicabs, and was a major figure in the numbers racket. Both Holzapfel and Lincoln became partners with Judge Peel. With his official protection they could prosper, and all he wanted in return was a cut, a big cut . . .

But in the spring of 1955 Judge Peel was in trouble again, after assuring a client that she was legally divorced. In fact she was not. The truth came out when she remarried and tried to adopt a child, only to discover that she was an unwitting bigamist. She made an official complaint. Peel had to appear before Judge Chillingworth again, on 15 June 1955.

This time Peel knew all his grandiose plans were threatened. So at 9.30 a.m. on 3 June, Peel contacted his good friend 'Lucky' Holzapfel. He told him: 'Judge Chillingworth is going to ruin me. We have got to get rid of the judge.' The three-way partnership between the judge, Holzapfel and Lincoln brought in thousands of dollars every week. But without the judge, the other two were out of business. It was agreed that for purely commercial reasons, Judge Chillingworth had to die. Bobby Lincoln was brought into the conspiracy to help Holzapfel commit the deed. The judge could hardly dirty his own hands.

Peel drove both men out to the Chillingworths' beach house and made sure they knew the layout. He also wanted them to observe the judge and make sure of recognizing him. On the night of 14 June – the day before Peel had to appear before the judge – Holzapfel and Lincoln drove to the Riviera Beach dock, Holzapfel wearing a jaunty yachting cap.

Boarding a small motorboat, the two men steered out into the night, following the coastline until they drew level with the beach house. They beached the boat at about 1 a.m. and walked up to the house. While Lincoln hid in the shadows, Holzapfel knocked on the door. When the judge appeared, Holzapfel took out a pistol and ordered him out on to the porch. Conscious of being exposed by the porch light, Holzapfel ordered Lincoln to break the bulb with his pistol butt, which he did.

Mrs Chillingworth came on the scene. She was unexpected, but Peel had warned both men that any witnesses would have to die too, as they would lead directly to the electric chair. The elderly judge and his wife were tied up and their hands taped behind them. On the steps leading down to the beach Mrs Chillingworth began to scream. Brutally and without hesitation Holzapfel pistol-whipped her; her blood spattered on to the steps. The couple were then forced aboard the motorboat and taken out to sea. It was not enough that they had to die: to satisfy Peel they had to *disappear*.

Both victims had weighted vests put around their waists, of the type used by scuba divers. As she was lifted on to the gunwale on the boat, the judge shouted to his wife: 'Remember, I love you!' She just had time to reply: 'I love you too' before being pushed over the side with a loud splash. She sank rapidly. The judge struggled at this point, trying to grapple with the men and managing to fall overboard. Even with his hands tied he managed to swim, after a fashion. His two killers followed in the boat, hitting him over the head with a shotgun butt when they were close enough. The butt shattered, the judge swam on. Finally, Holzapfel managed to grab him by the collar and tie the anchor to his neck, before pushing him away. The judge sank, to rest beside his wife. This sad and tragic tale is how it was done. Judge Peel had reckoned that without any bodies, there could be no case for a murder charge. Even judges fall victim to the myth of the *corpus delecti*.

Barely a month after these murders, Peel was suggesting to his two tame assassins that State Attorney Phil O'Connell should be the next victim: 'He has to be killed next. He is standing in the way of my political ambitions.' But this time the men demurred, and so no attempt was made on O'Connell's life.

Then came the Harold Gray insurance plot, which failed, leading to the arrest of Peel along with Holzapfel. Both men managed to extricate themselves from that debacle. However, Peel was finished as a judge and had to scrape a poor living as an ordinary lawyer.

Holzapfel, and Yenzer – the insurance agent – had, incredibly, become house detectives in the plush Deauville Hotel, although Holzapfel kept his moonshine business going in partnership with Bobby Lincoln. But more importantly, the entire episode had focused police attention on Peel, and on his unsavoury associates.

In due course Holzapfel and Lincoln murdered a rival moonshiner whom they suspected of having informed on them. They took Lew Gene Harvey for a ride into the countryside, before shooting him and putting his weighted body into a creek. This time the body surfaced. Sheriff Kirk now called in expert help from detectives in the capital, Tallahassee.

They sent Detective Henry Lovern, a slow-talking young man who chewed gum and seemed a bit of a country bumpkin. In reality he was a university graduate with a mind as sharp as a rat-trap. He had been fully trained in modern detection and forensic techniques. He began his investigation by hanging around Palm Beach, just listening. Merely by keeping his ears open he soon learned who was active in the moonshine racket. Ostensibly his job was to investigate the Harvey murder, but as more names cropped up, Lovern began to detect a *pattern*, and that pattern seemed to include ex-judge Peel, Holzapfel and Lincoln.

Remembering that failed insurance scam, Lovern made a point of contacting Jim Yenzer in Miami. The former insurance man was a bitter and soured man. When Lovern wanted to discuss the Harvey murder, Yenzer wanted to talk about the Chillingworth murders. Lovern pretended to be bored by this: it was all old stuff. But the less enthusiastic he appeared, the more eager Yenzer was to talk about the murder of a distinguished judge. He hinted that Peel had arranged the murders, and offered to work as an undercover agent, or informer.

Lovern feined a lack of interest. But he quickly contacted Sheriff Kirk and State Attorney Phil O'Connell, informing them of the new development. Everything Yenzer had said fitted the pattern of the Chillingworth case, and the senior men became excited at the prospect of a solution at last. Lovern was told to pretend to apply himself only to the Harvey murder, but was given permission to recruit Yenzer as an agent.

Lovern asked Yenzer to become friendly with Holzapfel again, since both had been involved in the failed insurance plot. The two men duly made contact and became firm friends, a mutual trust born of the fact that they were both bad men together. Yenzer encouraged Holzapfel to talk about the Chillingworth murders, and even helped him in a couple of crimes, having got Lovern's permission. In the second crime – the attempted hijacking of a shipment of arms, about which Yenzer had warned Lovern – the two men were ambushed by waiting police and Holzapfel was arrested, Yenzer being conveniently allowed to escape.

Holzapfel now needed $15,000 bail money to get out of jail. Half this money was put up by a bail bondsman who had once served as a police officer in Palm Beach. But before he left jail a free man, Lovern had established that Holzapfel was driving the same car Harvey had been driving when last seen alive. Lovern made no move. He was playing it very casually, giving his prey a long string, content to let the fish run in the hope they would bite on the hook in time.

By October 1959, Peel had set up a phony construction company in another part of Florida, called ICC, to take in the life-savings of pensioners with promises of a get-rich-quick scheme. One of his partners was none other than Floyd Holzapfel . . . Detective Lovern was aware of all this, but was simply not interested. Other authorities could take care of the fraud case; he himself was busy building up a case against the former judge whose charming exterior hid a cold-hearted murderer.

Then came a complication. In December 1959, Holzapfel was due to appear in court for the hearing of his appeal against his conviction and fifteen-year sentence for the attempted arms shipment hijacking. But he jumped bail, fleeing to Rio de Janeiro. The outraged bail bondsman, who stood to lose thousands of dollars as a result, began talking to the police. He knew something about Holzapfel's connections with Judge Peel. He too became an undercover agent. The State was moving slowly, but in the process it was building a strong case against Peel.

Holzapfel did not like life in Rio. He was almost permanently broke. Judge Peel sent him only dribbles of money from their joint company. He told his wife to see Judge Peel and tell him to send more money, or else . . . Judge Peel had suddenly found himself without friends. Even Bobby Lincoln was in prison, serving time for moonshining, and now Holzapfel was making threats against his life.

But Yenzer appeared to be a friend, and Judge Peel confided in him, offering him $5,000 to kill Holzapfel if he returned to Florida. It was a classic 'contract killing' offer. Yenzer promptly informed Lovern of the offer, and now Lovern turned Holzapfel's absence into an advantage. He got Yenzer to phone Holzapfel in Rio, telling him it was a shame Judge Peel wouldn't send him any money, since the company was making vast profits. He also hinted that Judge Peel was having an affair with Holzapfel's wife.

This infuriated Holzapfel enough to make him return to the States – as Lovern had planned. In September 1960 Holzapfel phoned Judge Peel from a Florida hotel, making threats. Peel in turn phoned Yenzer and told him it was time to execute the contract killing. Yenzer arranged a meeting with Peel in a hotel room to discuss the details, a room which Lovern had had thoroughly bugged. Everything Peel said went down on tape.

Peel asked Yenzer to kill Holzapfel quickly. There would be $5,000 waiting. Yenzer demurred, wanting half the cash in advance. The judge paid him $1,800, promising the rest once Holzapfel was dead. He himself, he said, would be leaving for Daytona to establish an alibi.

Now Yenzer phoned Holzapfel, asking for a meeting in the same bugged room. Once Holzapfel got there, Yenzer lost no time in telling him that Peel had paid for him to be killed. Holzapfel was murderously angry. He talked at length about the Chillingworth killings, complaining bitterly about what he had done for the ungrateful Peel. At this point armed officers burst into the room and arrested him.

Judge Peel was arrested on 4 October 1960 and was questioned by Phil O'Connell, who could not hide his disgust for the lawman turned killer. Peel refused to talk, but after a day in the local jail he sent for O'Connell and offered him a deal. In exchange for immunity from prosecution, he was willing to tell everything he knew. O'Connell, furious at the suggestion, told him to go to hell. Peel calmly reminded him that without any bodies and no witnesses, the State had no case. O'Connell's response was to charge Peel with conspiracy to kill Holzapfel, and have him lodged in jail. Bail was set at $25,000.

Peel managed to raise the money, and once at liberty he vanished, having given trailing detectives the slip. The authorities were left with Holzapfel in jail in Maine, and Bobby Lincoln in a Federal prison. They turned to them. Lincoln, frightened at the prospect of the electric chair, offered to talk if given immunity. Despite the complications this brought – at that time no white jury would convict a white man on the testimony of a black – O'Connell was inclined to grant immunity. But then Holzapfel began to talk without any inducement.

At a preliminary hearing he burst into tears and told the astonished judge loudly: 'People like us ain't fit to live. We should be crushed like cockroaches.'

Lovern, meanwhile, had discovered Peel's whereabouts: hidden away in a hotel in Chattanooga. Once again he arranged to have his room bugged. More incriminating conversation went on to tape. When he was ready, Lovern walked in and slapped handcuffs on Judge Peel, telling him laconically: 'Mr Peel, you just never learn to keep your mouth shut.'

Once in the local jail at West Palm Beach, Peel denied everything and told reporters that he was innocent and had been framed by O'Connell as an act of political revenge. Many were inclined to believe the handsome young former judge who had been so popular. That is, until the trial . . .

The trial was held at Fort Pierce, midway between Daytona and Miami, after Peel had complained he could not get a fair trial in Palm Beach. On 7 March 1961 – five years after the murder of Judge Chillingworth – Peel stood before Judge D. C. Smith in a fight for his life. O'Connell wanted that more than anything else. Peel's life. A burly man who was once a prize-fighter, he was determined to get justice for the dead.

Peel's position was not good. There had been adverse pre-trial publicity. Any jury could not fail to be aware that Holzapfel had pleaded guilty to first-degree murder in the Chillingworth case, thus sentencing himself to the electric chair. He was expected to testify against Peel; as was Bobby Lincoln, promised immunity and brought from jail for the occasion. There were also something like seventy hours of tape-recordings to back up the secondary charge of conspiracy to murder Holzapfel. But the main charge was the murder of Judge Chillingworth.

Phil O'Connell, the State Attorney who had given Peel a break by loaning him office space, now sought to destroy him, as prosecuting counsel in the case. Peel had a defence counsel, but gave him his own minute-by-minute instructions. In a sense Peel was both defendant and counsel in the trial.

Phil O'Connell began by declaring in his big booming voice: 'We intend to prove that the defendant, Joseph A.

Peel, Jnr. was a municipal judge in West Palm Beach. We will show that Peel had trouble with the late Circuit Judge C. E. Chillingworth prior to 15 June 1955. We will prove that Peel was engaged in the Bolita (numbers) and moonshine rackets with Floyd Holzapfel and explained he was about to be ruined. He said the judge had got to go. They got Bobby Lincoln, a Negro, into the picture and the trio scouted Chillingworth's beach home several times . . . We will show how Peel arranged for the boat in which the Chillingworths were drowned.' O'Connell paused to glare at Peel, his former friend, before he spat out: 'Peel and nobody else planned the killing of Judge and Mrs Chillingworth.'

Although American law is based on the English legal system of common law, there are many differences. For example, although Peel was on trial for just one charge – the murder of Judge Chillingworth – the prosecution were able to drag in many alleged crimes which had no relevance to the present charge, including the attempted murder of Holzapfel, Peel's involvement in the rackets, the attempted insurance scam, the murder of Harvey, and so on. Little of this would have been admissible in a British court of law. There was also an element of personal vindictiveness in the prosecutor. O'Connell was by turns sarcastic, scornful, contemptuous and bullying, often shouting his questions.

The defence counsel, Mr Welch, by contrast with the overbearing O'Connell, was a polite young man, if a little vague in his tactics. He was fighting a losing battle all the way. But by appearing as a bullied little boy, he won the sympathy of the jury. He began his opening statement by saying: 'After the Chillingworth disappearance, rumours began to circulate. Peel, blessed with natural qualities, entered Palm Beach County politics. He soon made enemies. Some of those enemies are now ready to testify against him in this court.' He added that O'Connell was more than the State Attorney; he was also political boss of Palm Beach County.

He said it was ridiculous to suggest that by killing the judge, Peel could have prevented the disciplinary action against him. The prosecution had no real case; they were using hoodlums to frame Peel, men who had everything to gain by lying. Bobby Lincoln, who had confessed to three murders, had been promised immunity if he swore away the life of Judge Peel. Yenzer was after the reward money of $100,000. But significantly, Mr Welch did not mention Holzapfel, who had nothing to gain by lying, and had indeed sentenced himself to the electric chair with his confession.

The prosecution admitted that it was using 'not very pretty people' and some underhand methods – secret tape-recordings, and informers who had acted as *agents provocateurs* – to convict Peel. But as O'Connell said with a tight grin: 'You can't go skunk huntin' in a tuxedo.'

On the third day of the trial Holzapfel, who had been brought from jail in shackles, testified against his former partner in crime. He glared malevolently at Peel before he was questioned. Peel would not meet his eyes. Speaking in a deep baritone voice, Holzapfel began by declaring his own guilt in the murders of Judge and Mrs Chillingworth and Lew Gene Harvey. Then he began dragging Peel into the electric chair with him.

He and Judge Peel had first met eight years previously, he said, and they soon became partners in the rackets. Peel used racket money to pay for his second election for municipal judge. Holzapfel was given the job of raising the money.

O'Connell asked: 'How were you to raise the money?'

A: 'I was to contact certain Negroes and others in the West Palm Beach area to raise money for his campaign, with the promise that he would protect their business after he won the election.'

Q: 'What were these businesses?'

A: 'Moonshine, Bolita, Cuba, and so forth.' Holzapfel was a godsend to the prosecution, who were the subject of discontent all over Florida because it did not seem fair that they had granted immunity to a Negro who had committed three murders, just to get Judge Peel. But Holzapfel was a white man, with no axe to grind. And he gave his evidence confidently and well.

He came to the Chillingworth murders, telling how he had called Peel 'crazy' when he first broached the subject of killing the judge. But after frequent talks over a month-long period, Peel had convinced him that 'squinty-eyed old bastard' had to be killed to protect their business. Bobby Lincoln was brought in to help Holzapfel commit the deed. Holzapfel testified that Peel had suggested the burial at sea of the victims: 'He said if no one could find the body, no one could be arrested.' Holzapfel then related the stark details of the actual killings, and how Judge Chillingworth had tried to swim away from the boat. 'Bobby started to shoot him, but I said, "No, Bobby, the sound of the shot would be heard." I started the boat and chased after Judge Chillingworth. Using an anchor we had in the boat Bobby held the judge by the side of the boat and I got a piece of rope and tied the anchor around the judge. Bobby let him go and he went down.'

Mr Welch cross-examined. Holzapfel admitted to a long criminal career – although at one time he had been a fingerprint expert for the police of Oklahoma City. He denied having committed the murders for money. He had never got a cent for the job. 'I did it for Joe Peel. I did it for friendship.' It was damning testimony. He could not be shaken in cross-examination. For two days he was hounded on the stand and confessed to being a liar, thief and murderer. A man who had served time in prison. But as for the guilt of Judge Peel, he was implacable. Peel had masterminded the murders . . .

On the sixth day the bail bondsman and former policeman took the stand. P. O. Wilber had a grating voice. He testified: 'I said to Joe Peel, why did you do the job on Judge Chillingworth?' and he said, 'It was either that son of a bitch or me.' Wilber had been in the rackets too, and had often put up bail for his friend Holzapfel, and had been a friend of Peel's. He admitted that he had worked undercover for the police, along with Jim Yenzer, to get evidence on Peel and share the reward money.

Various witnesses testified to Peel's involvement in the rackets, one Negro telling of how Judge Peel had personally promised him protection for a fixed weekly payment. Even when voted Man of the Year by the Junior Chamber of Commerce, Judge Peel had been heavily into corruption. Witnesses had seen Peel and Holzapfel counting huge amounts of numbers money on a table in the judge's office.

On the seventh day another black man testified. Edward Johnson had been a trusty in West Palm Beach jail at the time that Peel and Holzapfel were held there. One day Peel gave him a packet of cigarettes, and showed him an amount of white powder at the bottom of the packet. He said it was cyanide, and all he had to do was to sprinkle it on Holzapfel's food. 'Without him I can beat the Chillingworth case,' he explained. 'If you do it, you will be well taken care of.' Johnson had reported the matter to the warden. So even in prison, Peel had tried to kill Floyd Holzapfel . . .

Then came the matter of the incriminating tapes, the sounds of drunken men boasting, the oaths and swearwords of men at play. Peel could hardly deny his own voice. All he could do was to say he had been misunderstood. He had talked of killing Holzapfel, but only after the man had violently threatened him. It was almost self-defence.

Bobby Lincoln, a big man with a mean stare, testified. He too described his involvement in the Chillingworth murders, describing them almost exactly as Holzapfel had, except that in his version he had just watched as Holzapfel put the two victims over the side. It was he who had heard the judge say to his wife: 'Remember, I love you', and her reply. In his version, Lincoln had been an innocent witness to murder. He confirmed that Peel had ordered the killings. He left the court, having completed his part of the immunity deal. He would walk out of prison free after a year, despite having confessed to three murders.

It was on the twelfth day of the trial that Peel took the stand in his own defence. Mr Welch told the jury: 'This young man will have to bare his soul and his life before you.' It was a calculated gamble. Peel thought he could use charm to defuse the scorn of O'Connell, and in a sense it worked. With his smart charcoal silk suit, his air of sincerity, and those winsome smiles of his, he did charm some of the jury. But he could hardly combat the weight of all the evidence.

He denied having either directly or indirectly participated in the murder of Judge Chillingworth. He had never been involved with either Holzapfel or Lincoln in any criminal enterprise, including numbers rackets. Both had been former clients who had been persuaded to tell lies about him by either a vindictive prosecutor or the promise of reward.

'I never recall going out to dinner with Floyd Holzapfel. I never socialized with him. I had lunch with him two or three times, and I went to his house once.' Peel said that following the discovery of the body of Lew Gene Harvey in the second week of November 1958, 'Holzapfel telephoned me. He made some admission to me about the matter.'

He then recounted how, after quitting law, he was persuaded by Holzapfel to become a partner in a construction company. He accepted the position out of fear of Holzapfel. But following his flight to Rio, Holzapfel had become even more violent and abusive, making threatening calls. Peel said he had begun to feel frightened of the man.

O'Connell jumped up at this and said loudly and with a knowing look at the jury: 'He ought to be afraid of

Holzapfel. He paid eighteen hundred dollars to have him killed!'

In his cross-examination, O'Connell spat and growled at Peel, but made no headway. Peel just kept denying everything. O'Connell then called Henry Lovern to the stand. Lovern spoke of his work for the Sheriff's Bureau on the Harvey murder case, and his subsequent work on the Peel case. He had heard Peel beg O'Connell to give him immunity – something which Peel denied ever having requested. He was asked: 'Did you overhear the private conversation between O'Connell and Peel on 4 October 1960?'

A: 'Yes.'

Q: 'Would you relate it to the jury?'

A: 'I was immediately adjacent to the grand jury room in a small office. The door had a half-inch space at the bottom. I laid down on the floor with my ear next to that space. I could hear Joe Peel say: "Phil, they got me. They got me cold. Sometimes you win. Sometimes you lose. This time I have lost. I have got to have immunity." '

Q: 'Did he make those statements after Mr O'Connell asked him about the Chillingworth case?'

A: 'Immediately after. Mr O'Connell said he would never give him immunity in the Chillingworth case.'

On the sixteenth day prosecution and defence made their closing summations. Defence counsel said the case rested on shaky foundations and perjured witnesses. He stressed that O'Connell was desperate to put Peel in the electric chair, at whatever cost. 'They have three suspects. What do they do? Give Bobby Lincoln, confessed murderer of three people by his own testimony, immunity. They took a hardened criminal and let him off, just to get the judge . . . I want you to recall Joe Peel's testimony. He looked you in the eye. He didn't hide one thing. Not one thing. He was not shaken in his testimony.'

Mr Spellman, assistant prosecutor, spoke next. He

said: 'The court will instruct you that there are four elements that the State must prove beyond all reasonable doubt. The State must first prove the death of Judge Chillingworth. Second, that he died of a criminal agency. Third, that he was drowned by Floyd Holzapfel. Fourth, that Joseph Peel counselled, hired, persuaded and commanded Floyd Holzapfel to kill Judge Chillingworth.'

He then explained the details to the jury. If all three men had confessed to the murder, that would not prove the *corpus delecti* of the crime under Florida law. What was needed was a *witness*. Bobby Lincoln had been that. 'Why did we give that big, black murdering boy immunity? For the simple reason that, gentlemen, we have got to prove the murder of Judge Chillingworth. We have to have direct evidence to present to this jury. We could not bring back the body, so we had to grant immunity to get an eyewitness of what happened. Bobby Lincoln was that witness. He was just a tool, an employee of Holzapfel. Of the three men he is the most insignificant.'

Mr Welch spoke again – both sides were allowed two summations. He complained that the authorities had been out to get Peel, to entrap him by any method. He poured scorn on the testimony of Lovern – 'a man with photographic ears. He has the power to repeat verbatim a conversation between two men five months ago. Such a performance is unknown to science.'

Playing on the fears of the jury and trying to introduce some doubt in their minds, Mr Welch wondered aloud: 'What if it is found out at a later date that Judge Chillingworth did not die as alleged in the indictment, but that the body was found in a shallow grave some place – or not at all?'

He continued: 'This is all part of a plot for Floyd Holzapfel to seek revenge on this boy and take him to the electric chair with him . . . They have tried to blacken the Peel name. They want you to base your verdict on passion and prejudice and anxiety and fear.'

O'Connell had the last word. Standing bull-like, he

roared at the jury: 'I have lived since June fifteenth 1955 for this hour. The ghost of Judge Chillingworth walks tonight.' Pointing to Peel he said: 'Smart fella. Clever. But he walked in error. There is honour among thieves, they say. There ain't no such thing. They go huntin' for each other all the time . . . Joe Peel has the most warped mind I have ever known. Who corrupted who? Did Holzapfel corrupt Peel, who corrupted Bobby Lincoln? What does it matter?'

He pointed to Peel again. 'But this one was the brains. The leader. Peel made Bobby Lincoln the biggest nigger in Palm Beach. He walked big. He could say, "I got the judge in my hand," and prove it. Before that Lincoln was never convicted of a crime. Who made him a murderer? Joe Peel . . . Who do you think whispered in Lincoln's ear and made him a murderer? That fellow right there.'

Turning to Peel's attempt to have Holzapfel poisoned while in jail, O'Connell bellowed: 'If that had happened, Peel would have been home free. I believe that Joe Peel must forfeit his life to the state of Florida and I ask you for a verdict of guilty with no mercy.'

On the seventeenth day the jury retired, taking agonizing hours over their verdict. Finally they returned. 'We the jury find Joseph Peel guilty of being an accessory before the fact in the murder of C. E. Chillingworth and a majority of us recommend mercy.'

Joe Peel had escaped with his life. He could expect to be paroled after ten years of a life sentence. Holzapfel faced the electric chair, but was reprieved at the last minute, no doubt because of his aid in convicting the former judge. It was a sordid and dirty case, illustrating the typical corrupt underbelly of any American city and the cynical application of the law.

No doubt the authorities did use 'dirty' tactics to secure a conviction, but as O'Connell said: 'You can't go huntin' skunks in a tuxedo.' And once again a universal truth was demonstrated: it *is* possible to prove murder without a body . . .

7
LEONARD EWING SCOTT: EGOTIST AND WIFE-KILLER

The majority of criminals are feckless, immature individuals who commit crime on impulse and when caught admit their guilt freely and accept their punishment stoically. But there exists a small percentage of criminals who exhibit tremendous ego, who are clever and manipulative and believe they are superior to the police and can outwit the law. Time and again they are proved wrong, yet they persist. Ted Bundy was a typical example, a man who viewed murder almost as a challenge. But before him there was a long line of men who were convinced of their superiority.

They are basically individuals who are predators, viewing the world as a jungle, with the majority of people as prey. They tend to stalk and kill the weaker members of the tribe, hence they will typically select lonely women as their prey. George Joseph Smith – of the 'Brides In The Bath' infamy – made a career of this. This is the story of one such creature: Leonard Ewing Scott.

He was born in Missouri, USA, on 27 September 1896. Endowed by nature with good looks and a fine physique, he was later to turn these assets to good advantage. If Scott had one distinguishing trait, it was a desire to live well without working. Early on in life he noticed that certain professional men enjoyed good incomes without breaking into sweat, principally stockbrokers and investment counsellers. This was the area he targeted, honing his skills to that end.

Lacking a college education, Scott took a lowly office job which brought him into contact with financial advisers and consultants, and he studied them as assiduously as a method actor learning a role. He noted their mannerisms, their conservative dress, the technical terms they used and their general patter. Modelling himself on them, he always dressed soberly, with a gold watch chain draped across his waistcoat, and perhaps a silk handkerchief peeping from his breast pocket. In short, he became a confidence trickster, and the fact that he was a handsome man standing six feet four inches helped. After all, handsome men make the best and most successful rogues.

He knew that the best way of acquiring wealth without working was to marry it, and in 1937 he married Alva Brewer, daughter of a wealthy Canadian publisher who also had mining interests. Scott immediately gave up all pretence of working, joining his wife on world cruises and lounging around the farm bought for the couple by the bride's father. After five years they were divorced, Scott receiving a hefty financial settlement. He always said his wife had been an alcoholic, but didn't say if that was the reason he used to beat her so much.

The divorce suited Scott, who was now free and relatively well-heeled. The marriage had introduced him to many important business connections of the father-in-law, and Scott lost no time in exploiting his entry to the exclusive old-boy network. During World War Two he worked briefly in Washington for the Government, before being sacked for lack of application. He was later to boast of his 'top secret' Government post.

After the war he set up a construction company to cash in on the real-estate boom. It made a profit, although even here Scott cut corners. But he also dabbled in other odd business ventures, including inventing a hair restorer, which he attempted unsuccessfully to peddle, and a pesticide spray.

His money was running out as his schemes folded, and he was saved in 1949 when he met and married a woman whom he described to his friends as being 'a rich old widow', boasting that now he would be managing her money as well as his own. And she had plenty.

Evelyn Throsby Mumper was aged fifty-seven. Five feet six, with greying hair, she was always immaculately dressed and wore expensive jewellery which was in modest good taste. This slender, ageing widow had been married four times, inheriting large amounts of money from each of her husbands. A prudent woman, she kept detailed accounts of her finances in a ledger, and with shares and other holdings was worth around a million dollars. Although she kept a full household staff and pampered herself with beauty treatments and entertained well, she was essentially frugal with her money.

She liked to travel and had made many trips to Europe and South America, but always made a point of leaving a copy of her itinerary with her friends and with her lawyer, in case some urgent business cropped up which required her immediate attention. This last point was to become a crucial clue to her fate.

Her last marriage had taken place when she was fifty-four, when she married Norris Mumper. That was in December 1946, and he died in September 1948, leaving her over thirty thousand dollars in cash, as well as a large house and an extensive stock portfolio. She was now financially secure for the rest of her life, a society widow with a wide circle of friends.

But she was lonely and vulnerable, and it was at a dinner party given by friends that she was introduced to the tall, silver-haired Scott in his well-tailored suit. He was charming to Evelyn, flattering her outrageously and treating her with old-world charm, courting her over candlelit meals and generally sweeping her off her feet. In August 1949 Scott suggested a leisurely drive to northern Mexico. Evelyn agreed, and during the trip Scott proposed marriage. Evelyn accepted eagerly, and they were married twice, first in Mexico on 3 September 1949, and again two weeks later in a civil ceremony in Nevada. He was fifty-three, she fifty-seven.

Within weeks of the marriage, Scott began isolating Evelyn from her old friends, persuading her to sell her house in Pasadena and move to a new house in the exclusive suburb of Bel Air, some forty miles away. It was part of Scott's pattern, or system. He did not want old friends around to protect Evelyn from her own folly.

The house was at 217 North Bentley Avenue, Bel Air, southern California. It was situated in a wealthy neighbourhood of expensive homes with Mexican maids and Japanese gardeners, and probably a Rolls and a Mercedes in the garage. The interior of the Scotts' house was furnished with good furniture and expensive objects, and the couple had household staff, including a maid and a chauffeur-handyman. But Evelyn Scott found herself living in isolation with a man who was virtually a stranger.

Soon he had badgered her into turning her stock portfolio, rental property and bank accounts over to him, saying that since he was an investment broker himself, he could look after it better than anyone. In 1951 he began liquidating her assets, turning her shares into ready cash, which he kept in a safe-deposit box. He said that he was convinced that an atomic war would soon break out, and shares would be worthless. What value cash would have in such an event he didn't explain.

Scott was by now beating Evelyn. The live-in maid, Vera Landry, witnessed many of the rows and saw Evelyn with black eyes. They had moved into separate bedrooms, and once, when the maid dared question Scott about his treatment of his wife, he replied: 'I didn't marry Mrs Scott for love – just for her money.' Most of Evelyn's friends had noted her bruises, and were sadly aware that she had married a fortune-hunter. Scott had also engineered a split between Evelyn and her brother Raymond, who had taken an instant dislike to Scott and did not trust him. Scott also persuaded Evelyn to sack all the staff as an economy measure, including the maid, keeping on just the chauffeur. And he also persuaded her to make a new will.

By 1955 Evelyn – or Scott acting on her behalf – had sold all her holdings, putting the cash into ten accounts in eight separate states, with ten thousand dollars in each. It was now that Scott began hinting to Evelyn's friends that she was very ill and her mental faculties were failing – although she described herself at this time as being 'as fit as a fiddle'.

Scott had been talking of taking Evelyn on a motoring tour of Spain, and she seemed keen on the idea. On 11 May 1955 she entertained her friends at the Beverly Hills Supper Club to celebrate her sixty-third birthday, and she chatted animatedly about the forthcoming trip. On Monday, 16 May 1955, a car salesman called at the house by appointment to try and sell the Scotts a Mercedes-Benz 220-S sedan, priced at just under three thousand dollars. Scott, appearing to be the typical affluent business tycoon, haggled over the price, and the salesman promised to contact him on Thursday for a firm decision.

The salesman, Ulrich Quast, had arrived at 2.15 p.m. and gave the couple a demonstration drive, leaving them at about 4.30 p.m. The couple had discussed their plans for a long, leisurely motoring tour with him. He was the last known person ever to see Evelyn Scott alive.

The following day an unidentified male rang a local beauty salon to cancel Mrs Scott's appointment for that day – and all future appointments. On 19 May Scott visited the Westwood branch of the First National bank and emptied his wife's safe-deposit box, after some argument with bank staff. He produced a co-renter's slip giving him joint access to the box. Soon afterwards he opened two new accounts at two other banks. He also wrote to an insurance company asking them to cancel the insurance on his wife's jewellery and to send him the premium refund of a few dollars. Parsimony is the mark of the man who kills for money. George Joseph Smith ordered the cheapest funerals for his brides . . .

When the car salesman phoned on Thursday about the car sale, Scott told him brusquely that he had changed his mind. Instead, he took to driving his wife's car, which was newer than his own. Any friends who tried to phone Evelyn were fobbed off with stories that she was away 'travelling'. (He had such contempt for 'ordinary' people – Evelyn's friends – that he didn't even bother to try to lie to them convincingly. That contempt, that ego, was to be his downfall.) But when the cleaner arrived and asked where Evelyn was, Scott told her: 'My wife has been taken suddenly ill and she's gone away for treatment in the East.' He then gave away a few of Evelyn's old clothes, explaining: 'She won't be needing them any more.' Finally he sacked the chauffeur-handyman. He was now alone in the house. King of his own castle.

Evelyn had vanished on 16 May. On 14 June Scott booked passage aboard the *Coronia* liner, just a single cabin, explaining that his wife would not be accompanying him. On 16 June he phoned Evelyn's best friend, Mildred Schuchardt, who had been frantically trying to contact Evelyn with calls and letters, to tell her that he had been up all night with Evelyn and was worn out. 'Evelyn has been very ill, mentally and physically,' he said. 'I'm afraid I'm going to have to put her in a sanatorium.'

When Mildred asked to speak to Evelyn, Scott retorted: 'You can't. At this very moment she is standing naked in the middle of the bathroom with a whisky bottle in her hand, using obscene language.' Friends who tried to contact Evelyn after that got no answer. Scott had had the phone line disconnected.

Mildred visited the Bel Air house herself two weeks later, determined to see for herself what condition Evelyn was in. She spotted Scott looking at her through a window, but he refused to open the door to her. Mildred now contacted Evelyn's lawyer, Jim Boyce, expressing her concern about Evelyn's well-being. He made various attempts to contact Evelyn and trace her whereabouts, without success.

Meanwhile, on 28 July Scott entertained wealthy friends at a small dinner party in a club, telling one wealthy widow he had his eye on: 'My first marriage lasted five years, and now my second wife has left me.' Then the miserly Scott made a mistake. He wrote to one of Evelyn's friends, telling her that his wife had had a mental breakdown, and would she return any expensive gifts his crazy wife might have given her. The friend immediately contacted the Los Angeles District Attorney, S. Ernest Roll. He had already received many phone calls and complaints about the missing Evelyn, and assigned investigator Nick Cimino to check the case out. Discreet inquiries were made.

It was an astonishing ten months after Evelyn vanished that the police began to take an interest, principally because they had not been informed that she was missing, and Scott had not filed a missing-person report. They checked bank accounts, discovering that three accounts at three banks, each holding substantial amounts, had lain dormant for months. Yet traveller's cheques which Evelyn had bought in anticipation of her trip had recently been cashed. Copies of these cheques were obtained and the signature matched against Evelyn's. They were forgeries.

Scott was now interviewed for the first time. He described his wife as being an alcoholic, suffering from terminal cancer and a lesbian to boot. He said his wife had left him, taking with her the eighteen thousand dollars in cash she kept in two envelopes in her room. Scott said: 'It was May the sixteenth . . . She drove to

Westwood Village for some special kind of toothpaste she liked, and just never came back.' Yet cheques bearing her signature had been cashed after this date, with forged signatures. Even the cheque Scott used to book his cruise trip had been drawn on Evelyn's account. Extensive inquiries revealed that none of the money in the ten special accounts had been touched – how was Evelyn surviving without money? And as for that special toothpaste, a full tin was later discovered in her bathroom.

All this took time, and Scott carried on as normal, paying court to the wealthy widow. When she asked him why he didn't just divorce his errant wife, Scott replied: 'I'll never get a divorce. I'm just going to wait until she is gone seven years and then she'll be declared legally dead.'

The district attorney's investigation took several months. They had proof of fraud – but not of murder. Raymond Throsby, Evelyn's brother, was not so patient. In mid-November he waited outside the house and waylaid Scott, demanding to know where his sister was. When Scott tried to fob him off with excuses, Raymond accused Scott of having 'done away with her' and said he was going to bring in the homicide police.

Scott, with a new woman in tow, Marianne Beaman, a divorcee aged forty-two, booked into a hotel in San Diego; the woman signing the register as 'Mrs L. E. Scott'. By January 1956 Scott had proposed marriage to Marianne and she had accepted, although she knew Scott was still legally married to Evelyn. Their hotel bill was charged to Evelyn's account.

The police now decided to act. On the evening of 13 February 1956, Scott was arrested in the lobby of his club and driven to his home by investigator Cimino. He was questioned there from 10 p.m. that night until the following afternoon. The evidence against him was compelling: the forged signatures on his wife's cheques, Scott's embezzling of his wife's assets, his lies about her health and whereabouts. And why should she have left him, leaving all her money behind? He was invited to answer these puzzles.

Scott repeated that he had last seen his wife at about 4.30 p.m. on 16 March the previous year. But now he changed a vital piece of his testimony. He said it was *he* who had driven to fetch the toothpaste, and on his return found her gone. The questioning went on.

Q: 'Where is your wife?'
A: 'I don't know.'
Q: 'Have you ever tried to find her?'
A: 'No.'
Q: 'Why didn't you call the police?'
A: 'She's done this kind of thing before. She just takes off and never says a word about it to me.'
Q: 'Were you ever planning to look for her?'
A: 'I was going to wait a year until I started looking for her . . .'

He denied ever telling anyone that his wife was in a sanatorium, and refused to take a lie-detector test.

A casual search of Scott's desk had revealed a paperback book written by him under an assumed name. With the title *How to Fascinate Men*, the book was a guide for the *female* fortune-hunter. Typically, Scott never paid the printer's bill.

The interrogators finally left Scott alone, warning him to forget any plans about taking a cruise, since he was technically under arrest. Despite tight police surveillance, Scott went ahead with his plans for that cruise, however. He appeared to ignore all that was going on around him. Evelyn's brother had filed a court motion for control of his sister's fortune, which hit the newspapers and embarrassed the Los Angeles Chief of Police, who hadn't known about the Scott case. Angered, he assigned his own officers to lead an investigation – but Scott had dropped out of sight.

He had been busy. He had got himself a lawyer, Charles Beardsley, and on 8 March presented himself at the district attorney's office to answer any further questions. His lawyer answered all questions for him. Frustrated police officers had to let him go, afterwards conferring with J. Miller Leavy, a top prosecutor in the DA's office and an expert on circumstantial evidence cases – which was all they had.

Leavy had prosecuted the Caryl Chessman case in 1948 and the Barbara Graham case in 1953, sending both defendants to the gas chamber. To his disgust, an Oscar-winning film of the Graham case was made, starring Susan Hayward and called *I Want to Live*. Leavy was familiar with slick, smart criminals who displayed a twisted cleverness – just like Scott.

On 9 March Scott again presented himself at the DA's office, this time determined to answer questions himself and to plant red herrings. He said: 'When we were first married I thought I was Evelyn's third husband. It wasn't until years later that I found out I was number five or possibly number six. I wish to point out that all of her former husbands are now pushing up daisies – and *all* of them were cremated.' He went on to suggest that Evelyn might have gone back East, to live with a son from one of her marriages. Since all this had to be checked out, essentially he was buying time.

Asking Scott to account for cancelling the insurance on his wife's jewellery, the DA was careful to describe it in detail: a brooch with four large diamonds and eighty-six smaller stones, a white-gold wristwatch and a strand of pearls. Scott said, 'Those pieces all belonged to my mother. I gave them to Evelyn after we were married.'

'When were you married?' the DA asked.

'Nineteen forty-nine.'

'That's strange, then,' the DA mused. 'Your wife first insured these exact same pieces in nineteen forty-six.'

On 10 March the house in North Bentley Avenue was searched by police looking for either Evelyn's body or clues to her fate. Nothing was found in the house, but concealed in the neighbour's garden, close to the wall, were a partial dental plate containing five teeth, and two pairs of spectacles. The plate was identified by Evelyn's dentist, the spectacles by her optician. In Scott's incinerator were found metal snaps from a woman's undergarments.

Although this seemed devastating, the only real evidence against Scott was of fraud and grand theft. A judge had placed Evelyn's estate in the hands of a trustee, so Scott couldn't plunder it any more, and when he was eventually found he was handed a summons to appear before a grand jury hearing on 24 April to face fraud and theft charges. Papers found during the search of the house had revealed that Scott regularly used two aliases: Robert McDonald and H. Hunt. A paper search found a safe-deposit box rented to McDonald in a Beverly Hills bank, and the signature was a perfect match with Scott's own handwriting. The box had been opened by the police on 1 August 1955, but was found to contain only two envelopes full of sand.

On 25 April the police were forced to arrest Scott when it was discovered that despite the warning not to leave town, he had secretly purchased a high-speed car in which to flee the state. Fingerprinted and photographed at the police station, he was released on bail. On Friday, 27 April, Scott appeared before the grand jury and was indicated on thirteen counts of fraud, four counts of grand theft and nine counts of forgery. Released once again on bail, he gave a television interview in which he claimed the DA's men had savagely beaten him to try to extract a confession. In court the DA denied this, saying: 'It is a figment of Scott's imagination. His statement is in line with his pattern of lies consistently told to law-enforcement authorities since the investigation into the disappearance of Mrs Scott and her funds began.'

Then Scott vanished, forfeiting his twenty-five thousand dollars bail. His car was found abandoned with a bullet hole in the windscreen, in an attempt to fake his own death by foul play. Police searched for Scott nationwide, even alerting Interpol. On 16 October a secret indictment on one count of murder was added to the charges Scott faced.

In fact, Scott went to live in Canada for some months under a false name, but made the mistake of returning to the USA on 9 April 1957 to buy a new car in Detroit – because it was cheaper. On 15 April he was arrested by an alert immigration officer at the Canadian border while trying to drive his car back.

Scott was returned to the United States by FBI agents, and was held in jail in Detroit awaiting extradition to California. He waived extradition when he discovered that he faced charges of unlawful flight to avoid prosecution by Federal authorities, with a guaranteed jail term of many years. Scott was finally arraigned for murder at Los Angeles Superior Court on 21 May, but the court agreed to delay the trial for three weeks to allow Scott's counsel to prepare a defence. This new lawyer agreed to take on the case without any fee; instead, he opted for a slice of the book and film rights to Scott's life story – a film company had made a firm offer, and Scott said he wanted Ronald Coleman to play him.

The prosecution spent those three weeks studying case law of murder prosecutions without a body. The earliest California case was *People v. Alviso*, when Jose Alviso was convicted of shooting to death John Ruhland and burning his body beyond recognition in 1880. The court wrote:

> It is very seldom that a conviction occurs without positive proof of death, either by eyewitnesses of the homicide, or the subsequent discovery of the body; and while the general rule is clearly laid down, yet the authorities concede that there may be exceptions . . . instances of the human body being disposed of by fire, or boiled in potash, or dissolved in acids, rendering it impossible that it should ever be produced . . . It is clear that in such cases the *corpus delecti* may be proved circumstantially or inferentially.

There was another case in 1925: *People v. Clark*, and a 1951 decision in *People v. Cullen*. In all, there had only been five murder convictions without a body in California history. But J. Miller Leavy intended to rely on an English case, that of *Regina v. Onufrejczyk*. One which readers of this book will be familiar with . . . (See chapter five.)

At the grand jury hearing, Leavy opened his case by saying: 'Avarice is one of the most basic motives for murder. Scott is not the first fortune-hunter to marry an older wealthy woman, learn all he can of her resources, murder her and then appropriate them to his and younger women's use and, unfortunately, he will probably not be the last.'

He spoke of the evidence in the case which suggested that Evelyn Scott was dead, and of Scott's attempts to describe her as an alcoholic, mentally deranged and a lesbian. He told too of Scott's lies regarding her whereabouts. The grand jury had no hesitation in indicting Scott on a charge of murder, despite the missing body.

The trial proper was set for 7 October 1957. The prosecution intended to call 98 witnesses and offer 304 separate pieces of evidence in the course of the nine-week trial. And Marianne Beaman had agreed to testify against Scott. He had given her his wife's jewellery and had promised to marry her.

Monday, 7 October saw Scott in court, dressed in a grey pinstripe suit and looking confident. Judge Nye had got the prosecution and defence to agree to sever Scott's murder charge from the thirteen other counts of forgery and grand theft, since the jury might reach a compromise verdict: finding Scott guilty on the lesser charges and acquitting him on the murder charge. It took a week to select the jury of seven men and five women. Justice is not speedy in the United States.

Leavy began by describing Evelyn Scott to the jury, relating how this 'keen, intelligent woman' was last seen alive at 4.30 p.m. on 16 May 1955 by a car salesman. He went on: 'The charge against L. Ewing Scott is for the murder of his wife, Evelyn Scott. We will not produce any witnesses who saw either the body of Evelyn Scott or any portion of it. However, we expect to prove that after the defendant married Evelyn, he entered into a long, well-planned, preconceived plan of deliberation and premeditation to do away with Evelyn Scott and to appropriate her vast estate. We will prove with circumstantial evidence that Evelyn Scott is dead and that she came to her death by a criminal agency.'

One by one the witnesses were called. The bank teller who had sold Evelyn the traveller's cheques. Ulrich Quast, the car salesman. Evelyn's dentist, who identified her partial plate, found buried in the neighbour's garden – teeth without which surely Evelyn would never have appeared in public. Her optician. Witnesses who spoke of Evelyn's sanity. Her doctor, who had examined her shortly before she vanished and pronounced her 'a perfectly healthy woman'.

Evelyn's friends testified. Scott had told them variously that Evelyn had gone away; that she was in a sanatorium – one of only three in the East; that she was travelling in Spain, that she had gone to live with a son. Bankers testified to Scott's withdrawal of Evelyn's funds. Handwriting experts testified that he had done so with forged signatures on cheques. Piece by piece the jigsaw of circumstantial evidence the prosecution had assembled fell into place.

At the end of the prosecution case, defence counsel objected: 'We have here an unaccountable disappearance. Unless they can prove that Mr Scott had anything directly or indirectly to do with the disappearance, they haven't proved the *corpus delecti* . . . I don't believe Your Honour could preclude the good possibility of Mrs Scott returning to Los Angeles and into this courtroom . . . We have nothing but teeth, glasses, and a missing person . . . We are going to stretch the law too far if we are not careful.'

The defence called their witnesses, women who claimed to have seen Evelyn Scott long after she had vanished. They had bumped into her in a store, or passed her in the street, afterwards recognizing her from her photograph. There were at least three such witnesses, even one who claimed to have seen her at Mexico City airport, and another who sold her a train ticket to New York. The prosecution had little difficulty in discrediting these witnesses.

The defence scored with only one witness. Scott had claimed his wife was an alcoholic, her friends said she was not. But the chauffeur who had worked for Evelyn in 1936, Kenneth De Remy, said on the witness stand: 'Well, all I got to tell you is this. Her sobriety wasn't very good. She either had a mental aberration or she was drunk, that's for doggone sure . . .' But the witness himself was a confirmed drunk.

The prosecution in its final speech said: 'The law does not give a person a reward for disposing of his victim. Otherwise a person could kill and hide or dispose of his victim, then sit back smugly and be immune from prosecution . . . He was brainwashing Evelyn's friends for the day when he would murder his wife. He could then say she was ill and going to a sanatorium to account for the fact that she was no longer among us . . . It would be fantastic, impossible, ridiculous for this woman to walk out, to simply vanish voluntarily.'

The following day, Friday 13 December, the defence countered: 'If your husband or wife disappears, you had better stay home. Don't go anyplace or the district attorney will file a murder charge against you . . . I can't convince myself with all these witnesses that a crime of murder has been committed. I will defy anyone to find a *corpus delecti* unless there is a body someplace – whether you can see it or not.

'There is no violence in this case. They haven't told you *how, where, when* and *why*. You can't even visualize what is supposed to have happened to this woman. Tell me, what was his motive? You don't shoot Santa Claus.' Defence counsel reminded the jury how they would feel is they found Scott guilty, possibly sent him to the gas chamber, and Mrs Scott reappeared.

Scott did not take the witness stand, did not lay himself open to damaging cross-examination, a point the prosecution stressed, as they were then entitled to do. (The law was changed some years later.) Leavy hammered home: 'The defendant did not take this witness stand and and tell you with his own lips that he is not guilty!'

On Saturday, 21 December, the jury came back with a verdict, finding L. Ewing Scott 'guilty of first-degree murder as charged'. Scott merely coughed when he heard the verdict and remarked loudly to his counsel: 'I guess some people like Lincolns, and some people like Fords.'

The day after Christmas, in the penalty phase of the trial, Leavy argued passionately for four hours for the death penalty, saying: 'He has earned his sentence of death.' Defence counsel pleaded just as eloquently for Scott's life, and the jury responded to this, recommending life imprisonment. Judge Nye sentenced Scott to life in San Quentin.

Scott spent years exhausting the legal procedures of appeals, each time being turned down, the courts upholding the original verdict and proclaiming: 'The evidence of the appellant's guilt was convincing.' Even the United States Supreme Court refused to review the case.

Scott sent out a stream of letters protesting his innocence over the next few years, writing to anyone who would listen. In prison he was a hospital clerk for a time – a far cry from a broker. He wrote to all the Presidents: Eisenhower, Nixon, Reagan. It made no difference.

He was now an old man, and in November 1974 he was given a release date. He refused this angrily, saying that to accept parole was tantamount to admitting his guilt. But on 26 March 1978, aged eighty-one, he was literally pushed out of San Quentin, a free man. Finding a crowd of reporters waiting to interview him, he protested his innocence. He returned to Los Angeles to live in an apartment with a black and white TV, muttering darkly about suing the state to recover his fortune. And Evelyn's remains were never found.

Then, on Monday, 6 August 1984, Scott, now a querulous eighty-nine, phoned writer Diane Wagner and told her he was ready to give her his final interview. This interview was taped and formed the basis of Wagner's remarkable book, *Corpus Delecti.* (New York. 1986.) Scott told her: 'I did kill Evelyn.' He went on:

> 'I arrived in Las Vegas about dusk. I waited until it was dark and drove to a point six miles due east of the Sands Hotel. I began digging the grave. I got down about six feet, which was not any hard job in sand . . . I went to the car, I got the remains of Evelyn and dumped her in the hole . . .'
>
> 'How did you kill Evelyn?'
>
> 'I hit her in the head with a mallet, a hard rubber mallet. Just once, on the head, right on top. It was on that day we went for a test ride in the Mercedes Benz . . .'
>
> 'Why did you kill Evelyn?'
>
> 'Why? Because she tried to poison me, that's why. Isn't that a good enough reason?'
>
> 'Why did you decide to tell me all this about Evelyn?'
>
> 'Why did I tell you all this? Well, it makes a good story, doesn't it?'
>
> 'Is there anything else you want to tell me?'
>
> 'When I went before the parole board, before they had time to ask me any questions, I said: "Now, gentlemen, you are supposed to be here to do your duty, and I want you to answer me: Where is the *corpus delecti*? Because *corpus delecti* is the most important point, for the reason that until *corpus delecti* is established, there is no legal point in justice." '
>
> 'You thought if they never found the body, you would never go to jail? . . . You were just playing cat and mouse with them, to see if you were smarter than they were?'
>
> 'Well, I was smarter than they were, wasn't I?'

'Because you hid her body, and nobody ever found it?'
'Well, wasn't that smarter?'

For the reader there is one final puzzle: why, after years of protesting his innocence, did Scott finally confess to Diane Wagner? The reason is simple. He knew that death was near, and there is no point in having fooled everyone if no one ever learns of your cleverness. He remained an egotist to the end.

8

THE VANISHING OF MURIEL McKAY

Kidnapping was always traditionally an American type of crime. The gangsters of the twenties and thirties were very active in this sphere – 'Creepy' Alvin Karpis being a prime exponent of this activity. It had always been common in the south of Italy and in Sicily, and probably entered America along with the immigrants. The most infamous kidnap-murder was that of the Lindbergh baby, which resulted in the passing of the 'Little Lindbergh' law, making kidnapping a Federal offence and placing it under the jurisdiction of the FBI. From henceforth, kidnappers risked the electric chair. However, this did not prevent the later kidnapping of Frank Sinatra's son, or that of the grandson of billionaire Paul Getty . . .

Kidnapping never caught on in Britain. The British criminal may be every bit as ruthless as his foreign counterpart, but is perhaps a little smarter. Quite simply, kidnapping involves too many risks. There is the risk of the actual abduction, the risk of having to contact the relatives, the risk of picking up the ransom money without getting caught, and finally, the risk of returning the hostage.

It has been done. There was the kidnap-murder of heiress Lesley Whittle by the so-called 'Black Panther', Donald Neilson, in 1975, and more recently in the kidnapping of a female employee of an estate agents, but it was so unprecedented as to make national headlines, and the resulting publicity ensured a quick arrest.

However, not only is it a type of crime doomed to failure, but it is a squalid and messy business – on a par with child-abuse – which earns the contempt of all right-thinking major players in the cops-and-robbers show.

The kidnapping of Muriel McKay was Britain's first kidnapping for money, and consequently caught the police completely unprepared. They lacked the experience of handling such a case, and inevitably mistakes were made in the investigation; but it would be unfair to attach any blame to the police officers involved, who handled the inquiry in a totally professional manner.

If the crime can be said to have had a beginning, then the genesis of this kidnap plot lay in a television interview by David Frost in which he grilled newspaper tycoon Rupert Murdoch. Murdoch had been – and remains – a very successful and powerful newspaper baron in Australia. In 1968 he came to Britain, determined to become a leading player in Fleet Street, and after a bitter and prolonged battle with Robert Maxwell, he succeeded in gaining control of the *News of the World*. To boost circulation, he ran the memoirs of Christine Keeler for a second time, incurring the wrath of friends of Mr John Profumo and a rebuke from the Press Council.

The Frost programme was transmitted on 3 October 1969, in the course of which he referred to the many millions of pounds Mr Murdoch had spent to acquire a newspaper, referred to his young wife, and gave details of his lavish life-style. This resulted in Murdoch storming angrily out of the studio. But the programme had been seen by two men of Pakistani origin but from the West Indies, living on a remote farm in Hertfordshire, and made a strong impression on them. Here was an immensely rich man with an attractive young wife. Would he not pay a fortune to secure her safety? And so the germs of the kidnap plot were hatched.

Another Australian, Alick McKay, was also in the

newspaper business in London. He and his wife Muriel, both born in Adelaide – she on 4 February 1914 – fell in love as teenagers and eventually married. Alick McKay began working for the Murdoch organization in Australia, on the management side. He left in 1952 to join the Australian *Daily Mirror* group, and in 1957 was promoted to advertising director of the London *Daily Mirror*.

He and his wife came to England and looked around London for a house, finally buying a detached mock-Georgian mansion, St Mary House, at 20 Arthur Road, Wimbledon. They were a handsome couple, and Muriel McKay was fully supportive of her husband's ambitions. With her three children, she settled happily into the role of housewife, becoming a member of the local Tory party and getting involved with various charities. Her husband prospered; he was promoted several times and was awarded a CBE for services to exporting. He was now moving in exalted political and business circles.

In 1969, following a heart-attack scare, he retired with a golden handshake, but made a good recovery. Rupert Murdoch had that same year acquired the *Sun* newspaper, which was ailing at the time, and he was determined to make it Britain's biggest-selling national daily newspaper. He hired Larry Lamb as editor, and the newspaper thrived, eventually overtaking the *Daily Mirror* in terms of sales.

Murdoch realized that he needed to strengthen his management side, and in particular, he needed a right-hand man he could trust. He hired Alick McKay as a member of the board of the *News of the World*, making him number two. With a capable deputy now in charge of his newspaper interests in the UK, Murdoch felt able to return to Australia for a six-week holiday. He left Alick McKay in charge, and even gave him the use of his distinctive blue Rolls-Royce (registration ULO 18F). Murdoch departed on 19 December, and the following day Alick McKay began his routine as acting chairman. He arranged to be picked up every morning at his Wimbledon home by the company Rolls, driven to work, and then driven home again in the evenings. It seemed an obvious and practical use of a company 'perk', but it was to spell doom for Muriel McKay.

The two men who had watched the Frost programme in a Hertfordshire farm were brothers: Arthur and Nizam Hosein. Both had come from a Muslim culture in Trinidad. Arthur Hosein, aged thirty-three and the elder brother, seems to have been the dominant influence. He had arrived in Britain in September 1955 as a student, telling everyone he met that his ambition was to become 'a country gentleman and a millionaire'.

This was a far cry from his childhood spent in a wooden shack in Trinidad, among the sugar cane fields. Born on 18 August 1936, Arthur was determined to make his future in Britain, despite the racial prejudice he met with. He had spent fours years being taught tailoring by his strict father, and it was a skill he was to exploit later. First came the inconvenience of finding himself liable for National Service. He was called up to the Royal Pioneer Corps, but soon went absent without leave and in 1960 was court-martialled for desertion. He got six months in the military prison at Aldershot, to be followed with a dishonourable discharge. His commanding officer had told the court: 'He is immeasurably the worst soldier it has been my misfortune to have under me . . .' But as he was led away to the cells, Arthur Hosein shouted defiantly to the officers of the court: 'Watch how you go with me. I'll be worth a million one day.'

Following his discharge, he married a woman of German origin and settled in the East End of London as a tailor. By 1965 he had become remarkably successful, and was generally regarded as being 'the best trouser-maker in the business'. He was earning enough to buy a comfortable semi-detached house, and in 1967 he began the initial moves to cement his ambition of being a country gentleman. He began proceedings to purchase Rooks Farm, by the village of Stocking Pelham, in Herts. Although only forty miles from London, it might as well have been on the dark side of the moon. The farm lay in bleak, deserted countryside, with a tiny village boasting just one pub. Arthur Hosein bought the ten-acre farm for £14,000, putting down £5,000 as a deposit. Two years later Arthur's younger brother Nizam, who was twenty-two and had convictions for violence in Trinidad, arrived in England, joining Arthur at the farm. He was given pocket-money and cigarettes in exchange for his labour, sharing the farmhouse with Arthur, his wife, and their two children.

The farm had a number of outbuildings, including three piggeries, a barn and several sheds. Arthur bought some pigs, calves and chickens, leaving his wife to look after the animals. He also had two vicious Alsatians which he kept chained as guard-dogs.

Arthur Hosein now bought a dark-blue Volvo car on hire-purchase, (registration XGO 994G) which was to feature in the kidnap plot. He also tried to play the part of the feudal lord in the village pub, boasting of his wealth and important connections. The locals ignored him, contemptuous not of his colour – as he imagined – but of his arrogance. And in his farmhouse, as lord of his own manor, Arthur watched the Frost programme, learned of the vast wealth of Rupert Murdoch, and laid his plans.

On 13 December 1969 his wife and children left to go on holiday in Germany, planning to return on 3 January. Alone at the farm, the two brothers began the first stages of their plan. The first problem was a ridiculous one: they simply could not find out the home address of Rupert Murdoch. It was not listed in the telephone directory. So they kept watch on the headquarters of the *News of the World* and watched the 'boss' being driven away in the Rolls. Nizam was sent to County Hall, Westminster, telling a clerk in the vehicle registration department that he had had an accident with a Rolls-Royce, registration ULO 18F and wanted to trace the owner. Nizam Hosein filled out the formal inquiry form in the name 'Sharif Mustapha', giving a cousin's address in Norbury. The answer to his query was that the Rolls belonged to the *News of the World* organization, which was of no help. The brothers decided to follow the company Rolls and see where it took the newspaper magnate at the end of a working day.

They duly followed the Rolls to the house in Arthur Road, Wimbledon, not even noticing that the man sitting in the rear of the vehicle was not Rupert Murdoch. By a tragic twist of mistaken identity, Muriel McKay was to be abducted by two desperate bandits who believed her to be the wife of Rupert Murdoch. It was a blunder typical of the amateur nature of the brothers' criminal enterprise.

The Monday of 29 December 1969 began as a routine day. The company Rolls picked up Alick McKay at 9.30 a.m. and Muriel waved her husband goodbye. Later, she went out in her own car to pick up her home help, and the morning was spent preparing the evening meal. At noon she went to Wimbledon village to do some shopping, buying an expensive outfit at a boutique, before returning home.

Muriel had an afternoon dentist's appointment, which she kept, returning home at five o'clock. She drove her help home, stopping briefly to buy two newspapers. It was five-thirty by the time she dropped off the home help, arriving back at St Mary House about ten minutes later. She put her car in the garage, then went inside the house to make a cup of tea.

The house had been burgled three months previously, as a result of which a chain had been fitted to the front door, which opened on to a hallway and lounge, with a kitchen and dining room beyond. Muriel switched on the television to watch the evening news, while she sat in a comfortable armchair scanning the newspapers. What happened next will never be known. But between this time and her husband's arrival home, she was abducted.

A neighbour who passed the house at about 6 p.m. did see a 'dark-coloured car' parked in the drive, but thought nothing of it. It is obvious in retrospect that this was the dark-blue Volvo belonging to Arthur Hosein.

Alick McKay returned home at his normal time of 7.45 p.m. He rang the doorbell for his wife to release the safety-chain, but was surprised to find the door unlocked and the chain off. As soon as he entered the house, Alick realized that something was badly wrong. His wife's handbag lay open, its contents scattered over the stairs. Going further inside, he noted that the telephone had been disconnected from the wall and was lying upside down, its number disc having been removed. On a nearby table lay a tin of sticking-plasters. On a chair was a bale of thick twine, and lying on the desk was a rusty bill-hook with a wooden handle. Lying on the floor were his wife's reading spectacles.

Immediately alarmed, Alick seized the bill-hook and ran upstairs, calling his wife's name, fearful that the intruders were still in the house. He came back downstairs slowly, puzzled. Had his wife simply gone out somewhere on an impulse, or had she been abducted? He checked further. When he discovered that his wife's jewellery was missing, together with a quantity of cash, he knew that the only explanation for his wife's vanishing had to be a sinister one.

It was at eight o'clock that he phoned the police from a neighbour's house. Ten minutes later a uniformed inspector arrived on the scene, and was quickly satisfied that a serious crime had been committed. He sent for CID reinforcements.

Detective Sergeant Graham Birch answered the summons, aware of the importance of the McKay family, of

Alick McKay's powerful contacts in the newspaper industry, that he was a man to be treated with great care and respect.

Alick McKay greeted him with the words: 'My wife is gone. What has happened? Where has she gone?' He took Birch inside the house, showing him the evidence of some kind of struggle, then showed him the front door, suggesting it must have been forced. The officer could see no marks suggesting this . . .

It was unfortunate that Sergeant Birch was not more familiar with the temperament of a different class. He was immediately struck by Alick McKay's calm manner, and could not believe that a man whose wife had been apparently abducted would be so self-controlled. In short, the detective was suspicious.

Birch explained later: 'The scene looked very much as if it had been set up for an amateur production of an Agatha Christie thriller. The keys and other oddments from the handbag dribbled down the stairs like neat rows of confetti.' Even the upturned phone worked perfectly well when pushed back into its socket. Birch's first reaction, and one supported later by more senior detectives from Scotland Yard, was that the scene had been set by Muriel McKay who, like many women before her, had wanted to disappear in a 'theatrical' manner. (Agatha Christie herself had disappeared for a period in very much the same fashion.)

Consequently, Birch asked Alick McKay about the state of his marriage, seeking a clue as to why his wife should desert him. Perhaps there was a secret lover in the background . . . He suggested tactfully that Muriel might have left of her own choice, a symptom common in many middle-aged women. Alick McKay reacted angrily to this suggestion. 'No. I know my wife better than that,' he replied.

This attitude – that the wife might have left voluntarily – coloured the police inquiry and caused an initial delay in the investigation. The theory that Mrs McKay might have disturbed a robber, for example, was discounted immediately because the scene was just too *neat*. Instead, the police concentrated on finding out if Muriel had a lover, or had been taken ill. Detectives later admitted that their first impression on that first night was that 'the whole thing smelt'. They even entertained the possibility that it was some press stunt to boost circulation.

This was strengthened when Alick McKay rang Larry Lamb at the *Sun*, telling him what had happened. Lamb immediately sent a reporter and photographer to Arthur Road. Soon the scene outside the house was of a crowd of uniformed officers holding back a mob of eager reporters. Strained relations between the police and the press were to sour the whole inquiry.

Alick McKay was questioned for most of that night and treated almost as a suspect. He had wanted as much press publicity about his wife's disappearance as possible, thinking it might help. For their part, the police wanted a complete press black-out. This essential conflict dogged the case. As a compromise, the police agreed that a short statement be issued to the Press Association.

Sergeant Birch went off duty at midnight, having alerted his superiors to what was going on. He was relieved by Detective Sergeant White. By now the press was putting pressure on Scotland Yard to act. Then, at 1.15 a.m., the telephone rang at St Mary House. Alick McKay's son-in-law, David Dyer, picked up the receiver, expecting it to be yet another reporter anxious for news. Instead, a male telephone operator spoke, saying he was putting through a call from a kiosk at Bell Common, Epping. A muffled voice – obviously disguised – said: 'Tell Mr McKay it is M3 – the Mafia.' Dyer motioned urgently for Alick McKay to pick up the phone, indicating that Sergeant White should listen in on the extension in the kitchen. The conversation then went on:

Caller: 'This is Mafia Group 3. We are from America. Mafia 3, we have your wife.'

McKay: 'You have my wife?'

Caller: 'You will need a million pounds by Wednesday.'

McKay: 'What are you talking about? I don't understand.'

Caller: 'Mafia – do you understand?'

McKay: 'Yes, I have heard of them.'

Caller: 'We have your wife. It will cost you one million pounds.'

McKay: 'This is madness. I haven't got anything like a million.'

Caller: 'You had better get it. You have friends. Get it from them. We tried to get Rupert Murdoch's wife. We couldn't get her, so we took your wife instead.'

McKay: 'Rupert Murdoch?'

Caller: 'You have a million by Wednesday night, or we will kill her. Understand?'

McKay: 'What do I do?'

Caller: 'All you have to do is to wait for the contact. That is for the money. You will get instructions. Have the money, or you won't have a wife. We will contact you later.'

Even now the police did not take the possibility of kidnapping for ransom seriously. At first they thought the call was a hoax. No genuine kidnapper would have made the call through the operator, instead of using the untraceable STD system. It seemed a naive act for a professional Mafia team – or any other professional criminals. The call could even have been the work of a Fleet Street hack with a sick mind . . . The police took no steps to record any more calls, never seriously expecting any further ransom demand. And the phone *did* remain silent for the rest of the night.

The whole plot went disastrously wrong from the start, because of the essential stupidity of the Hosein brothers. They did not think to leave a written ransom demand at the scene – which would have caused the police to take it seriously from the outset – and they were in the farcical position of being unable to ring McKay because his line was constantly blocked by reporters.

The newspapers for Tuesday, 30 December all made mention of the case; MYSTERY OF THE PRESS CHIEF'S MISSING WIFE, was the *Sun* headline. After a sleepless night, Alick McKay was beginning to show the strain, looking grey and haggard.

Commander Guiver from Scotland Yard had now taken charge of the inquiry, with Chief Superintendent Smith and Inspector Minors from Wimbledon directly under him. They had arranged for an official description of the missing woman to be circulated to all forces. It read: *Muriel McKay. 5 ft 9 ins, medium build, dark complexion, dark brown hair, straight nose, green eyes, oval face*. They also decided to release details of the ransom demand to the press, but deleted any mention of Rupert Murdoch's wife having been the intended victim. Crank calls began flooding into Wimbledon police station as a result, jamming the switchboard. Extra lines had to be quickly installed.

The immediate task was to set up a 'crime index', listing all clues and cross-referencing all information on the case. This task fell to Detective Sergeant Jim Parker. All statements from witnesses had to be added to the index. Among these was one from the male telephone operator who had put through the call from Epping. He said the voice had sounded 'American or coloured'. Another important witness statement, taken routinely among hundreds of others, was from a local resident who had been driving from Wimbledon towards Putney on the afternoon of 29 December. At 4.40 p.m. he overtook a Volvo and saw two men talking inside. One was of 'tanned Arab colour'. But there were 33,000 Volvos on British roads at the time. This information was filed in the index as 'Volvo' in one section, 'two men' in another.

Commander Guiver, an officer with a long record of success as a detective, was baffled by the case. He was to say: 'It was the most bizarre crime I had ever been faced with. Usually you have a starting point – a body, a weapon or stolen property. Here we had nothing, as the amount of jewellery taken was really insignificant. It just didn't look like a robbery: the place was too tidy.'

A thorough search of the garden and attics of St Mary House took place. The husband was still a suspect. Two detectives were stationed permanently at the house, and now a recording device had been attached to the phone – twenty hours after Mrs McKay went missing. But it had not come from official channels, which would have taken weeks. One of the detectives used his own portable machine.

At 4.59 p.m. the phone in the house rang again, and pips sounded as coins were pushed into a call box. The same voice said: 'Your wife had just posted a letter to you. Do co-operate, for heaven's sake. For her sake, don't call the police. You have been followed. Did you get the message? Did you get the money?' The phone then went dead. Most police officers on the case were now convinced that it was a genuine case of kidnapping, but some remained sceptical.

That evening the daughter of the missing woman went on television to make an impassioned appeal for her mother's return. The police did not welcome the additional publicity, feeling that the case would have been better served by secrecy. But even the Home Secretary was taking a personal interest. There was to be no sleep for the senior officers leading the hunt.

On Wednesday, 31 December, a letter was received at St Mary House. Postmarked '6.45 p.m. 30.12.69. Tottenham N 17', it was addressed to Alick McKay. Inside was a piece of lined writing paper of a cheap variety, across which was written in a faltering hand: *Please do something to get me home. I am blindfolded and cold. Please co-operate for I cannot keep going. I think of you constantly and the family and friends*. It ended: *What have I done to deserve this treatment? . . . Love, Muriel*. Alick McKay recognized immediately the distinctive handwriting of his wife. There could be no more doubts or procrastination. There was now a deadly serious hunt to secure the release of Muriel McKay and the capture of her kidnappers. The problem was: which had priority?

The American experience of kidnapping would have been useful here. The FBI agent is instructed that the safe return of the victim is his primary concern. For that reason, the FBI will often step out of a case to allow the family to pay ransom money, returning to it later to catch the kidnappers. From experience, they know that the first four days are crucial. That time can be used to make a deal with the kidnappers, but any newspaper revelations will scare the abductors off. 'The less publicity the better,' the FBI states. They also believe that after four days, the chances of getting the victim back alive are virtually nil. It took the police in the McKay case six and a half weeks to arrest the Hosein brothers . . .

There was simply too much publicity. The family enlisted the help of the Dutch clairvoyant Gerard Croiset. A photograph of Muriel McKay and a map of London and the suburbs were taken to him at his home in Utrecht. Amazingly enough, he was able to say: 'I see her being held at a farm.' He warned bleakly: 'If she is not found within fourteen days, she will be dead.' The police certainly did not welcome his help, even though it did lead them to a farm on the Essex-Hertfordshire border. The real farm, the Hoseins' farm, was just a few miles further on . . .

For a couple of days nothing more was heard from the kidnappers. Then the phone rang with another message from 'Mafia 3'. Again the demand for one million pounds was made. This time detectives thought the voice sounded 'Jamaican'. (Two separate 'fakes' were later to make demands for money, claiming to be the kidnapper. Both were arrested, and one was jailed.) Some progress was being made: the forensic lab at the Yard had come up with a fingerprint on the first letter written by Muriel McKay.

The police now decided to make the press work for them, briefing Alick McKay on what to say at a press conference on Saturday, 3 January. He was to put out the story that his health was very bad, and plead with the kidnappers to ensure that Muriel got her daily injection, vital for her health. It was merely cortisone for arthritis, but the police hoped it might lure the kidnappers into going to a chemist for the drug. Unfortunately, Muriel McKay was probably already dead by this time.

Alick McKay ended the press conference by issuing a statement to the kidnappers saying:

> I ask whoever is holding Muriel to get in touch with me immediately and let me know exactly what they want. If it is money, then I must know how and where it can be exchanged for my wife. In order to be certain I am dealing with the person who is holding Muriel, I must have positive proof that she is safe.

It was a police ploy to persuade the inept kidnappers make contact.

On Saturday 10 January another letter from the kidnappers, on the same cheap lined paper, was received by the *News of the World*. It said that once the police had left the McKays' house, they would contact Alick McKay with further instructions. Several words were misspelled, including 'existance' and 'occassion'. The writer complained that he had tried to telephone St Mary House many times but had failed to get through because the line was always engaged. This letter went to the forensic lab for analysis, and proved to be a vital clue.

On Wednesday, 14 January, the editor of the *News of the World* took a call from 'M', believing it was the head of SIS. The caller then identified himself as 'M3' and asked the editor to 'tell McKay to get a million. I have proof of her existence'. Later that day Alick McKay took a call from the same man. Another call came on 19 January. Alick McKay reacted emotionally, and detectives decided that he should take no more calls. That task was delegated to his son, Ian McKay. Getting emotional and dominating the conversation did not help the police; the idea was to get the kidnapper to talk at length, to draw him out.

At this time senior detectives sat down with Alick McKay and told him that their opinion was that Muriel was now dead. The prime objective now was to catch her killers. Although unwilling to believe what the officers said, Alick went along with their suggestions. There were more calls making the one-million-pound demand. On Thursday, 22 January, two letters and a phone call came to the house. The two from Muriel proved that she was dead. It was obvious that the kidnappers had forced her to write several letters in the early days, which could be sent out later as if she were alive. But the letters had been sent out of order; they referred to events of weeks previously, such as having seen her daughter on the television – but that had been on 31 December . . . One of the letters, definitely in Muriel's handwriting, began: *I am deteriorating in health and spirit . . . I'm blindfolded and cold . . .* The letters also contained the long-awaited ransom instructions, telling Alick Mckay to drive in his wife's Capri to a certain telephone box to await further instructions.

After some haggling, and another letter from Muriel – her last – received on Monday 26 January and reading: *You betrayed me by going to the Police and not co-operating with the M3 Gang . . . Love Muriel*, the final instructions were enclosed. The ransom demand read: *I am sending you final letter for your wife reprieve, she will be executed on 2nd February 1970 unless you keep our business date on 1st February without any error . . .*

On the 4d stamp on the envelope, scientists recovered the left thumb print of Arthur Hosein.

The envelope contained three pieces of material cut from Muriel's clothing and shoes. The police now arranged with a printer to run off fake banknotes. Top-security measures were set in motion, with 180 policemen and 56 unmarked cars being reserved for the operation. On Friday, 30 January, the kidnappers rang again to confirm the final details of the ransom drop. Ian McKay took the opportunity to say he could not use the Capri as the press would recognize it. Instead, he would arrive in the Rolls, with a chauffeur driving. The caller accepted this. In reality, two police officers with two-way radios would be occupying the car.

On Sunday, 1 February, the Rolls set off at 9 p.m., driving through the dark streets to the prearranged phone box. There the caller directed them on to another call box. Once there, the officers found a cigarette packet with a list of instructions signed M3. They were to drive along the A10 to a village called High Cross, and past that until they saw two paper flowers on a bank at the roadside, near Dale End. They were to leave the money there, then return to the first phone box to learn where Muriel was.

The Rolls drove along, followed by an unlikely bunch of trailing policemen – four of whom were dressed as Hell's Angels on motorbikes. Further back were cars containing 180 detectives. And the site of the drop had been smothered with detectives hiding in ditches and keeping watch. They were duly spotted by the Hoseins, who grew suspicious and avoided the trap. But an officer had been writing down the registration numbers of all cars which passed the spot that night. A Volvo 144 belonging to Arthur Hosein was noted. The operation was called off, a humiliating fiasco, but later, detectives visited houses near the drop-off site to see if anyone know of any West Indians living in the vicinity. There was none, but the local station sergeant mentioned two

Pakistanis who lived on a farm at Stocking Pelham. Detectives made discreet inquiries, discovering that a blue Volvo was registered to Mrs Hosein, but were satisfied that the Hoseins were a normal part of the scenery. A Volvo had now appeared in the crime index three times: at Wimbledon, later that afternoon in the vicinity of the house, and now in the ownership of the Hosein family. But the vital connection was never made.

At this point the family had given up hope, but the police coached Ian McKay as to what to say in the remote possibility of a further call from the kidnappers. Incredibly, it came a few hours later, the voice on the phone saying that M3 had spotted the tailing police around the Rolls, adding: 'The boss laughed and said he had seen cars around the pick-up spot.' Ian protested that the police had staked out the area without his knowledge or consent. This explanation appeared to be grudgingly accepted, although the caller said that in future he would only speak to Alick McKay, adding that he was going to plead for Muriel's life with other elements in the gang whom he called the 'semi-intellectuals'. He went on: 'I am fond of her – your mum – you know. She reminds me of my mum.'

Further arrangements were made with Alick McKay for the ransom to be paid; the call with the details came on Thursday, 5 February, the drop to be made the following day. The police had less than twenty-four hours to make their arrangements. Once again the same routine of using different call boxes was carried out, but this time the Rolls was shadowed by a helicopter. Two armed police officers sat in the front of the Rolls, another armed officer was locked in the boot. However, the officers were told to abandon the car at Theydon Bois, and take the underground to Epping. Once there, they were to take a taxi to Bishop's Stortford, and place the suitcases containing the money next to a car parked at a garage there. This was done; the garage had been put under observation by other detectives before the money arrived. The money was never picked up; those officers hiding in the background had been spotted.

However, an officer detailed to jot down the registration numbers of all cars which passed by did note a dark-blue Volvo, XGO 994G, which passed slowly by the money three times in the next two hours. The occupants seemed to stare at the suitcases. It had also been seen on previous days near the garage, and now the link was made. It was decided to raid the Hosein farm the following day.

It was at eight o'clock on a gloomy Saturday morning that a convoy of police vehicles containing twenty officers arrived at the farm with a warrant to search for Muriel McKay's jewellery. Arthur Hosein did not seem at all disconcerted by this police interest in him. He said cheerfully: 'I know nothing. I earn over £150 a week. I do not deal in stolen property. You can look where you like.'

The police did not find any sign of Muriel McKay or her jewellery. But they did find an accumulation of clues pointing to the guilt of the Hosein brothers. There was a tin of Elastoplast similar to the one left at the McKays' home; paper flowers similar to those left as a marker by the roadside for the money to be dropped off; and from Nizam's bedroom, an exercise book with lined paper similar to that used for the letters from the hostage and kidnappers. Forensic examination revealed marks on this paper linking it to the letters from Muriel McKay. There was the tear line, the position of the staples, and even the impression of some words which had gone through to pages further on in the book, including the words: 'St Mary' – the start of the McKays' address. And of course, there were the fingerprints, from the ransom letters and the stamp on the envelope.

Police also found a sawn-off shotgun which had been fired recently. A neighbour had heard a gunshot from the farm around New Year's Day. The brothers said they had chopped up a calf over the Christmas period to feed to the pigs, using a bill-hook for this purpose. But a neighbouring farmer said he had loaned Arthur Hosein a hacksaw; when it was returned on 1 January it was completely blunt. And in Nizam's trouser pocket was a piece of paper bearing the registration number of the car the ransom money was to be dropped by. It was classic circumstantial evidence – but it was enough.

Driven away to different police stations, the brothers were questioned separately for three days before being charged. Neither gave anything away. Nizam did attempt to kill himself by first jumping out of a window, and then banging his head against his cell wall. He was placed under constant observation. Arthur talked all right, but said nothing to implicate himself. He was conceited and arrogant, telling Chief Superintendent Smith: 'You have a very difficult case. I want to help you. I know this is an important case. It's worth a lot of money, isn't it? I mean the press. They would pay a hundred thousand pounds for the full story, wouldn't they?' At a further interrogation he even boasted that after his acquittal, he planned to make a film of the case, getting Richard Burton to play Smith, Frank Sinatra for the judge, and Sammy Davis Jnr for himself.

Nizam reacted quite differently to questioning. He trembled and began to cry, putting his arms around a detective and saying: 'Oh my! What has Arthur done to me? I want to die. Let me die. Kill me. Arthur always gets me into trouble. Kill me now.'

On remand in prison, Arthur once beat Nizam up on exercise, apparently to keep him under control.

The farm was searched over a period of many months by hundreds of officers; not a single trace of Muriel McKay – or even evidence that she had ever been there – was ever found. At the trial it was suggested that her body had been dismembered and fed to the pigs . . .

The trial of the brothers began at the Old Bailey on 14 September 1970, still without any evidence of a body.

The Attorney-General, Sir Peter Rawlinson, prosecuted for the Crown, telling the jury that if there was an 'irresistible inference' that the brothers were the kidnappers of Muriel McKay, then they must also have been responsible for her death. Stressing premeditation of murder, he said that from the moment the brothers burst into Muriel McKay's living room 'her death-warrant was signed'. Yet no one can seriously believe that the brothers intended to kill their hostage from the outset.

The brothers sat in the dock, Arthur, thirty-four, small and dark, but obviously dominant; Nizam, twenty-two, tall but nervous, as the prosecutor listed the evidence which pointed to their guilt. Handwriting experts were to testify that Arthur Hosein had written the ransom notes – from paper torn from an exercise book found at the farm. That rusty bill-hook found at the McKays' house was identified by a farmer who had lost it at Rooks Farm. And one piece of evidence which was incontrovertible: the fingerprint of Arthur Hosein found on the letters written by Muriel McKay.

Sir Peter Rawlinson, referring to the fact that the brothers had been seen on three occasions slowly passing the suitcases containing the ransom money, said it had been 'like a crow around its meat'.

Through his counsel, Douglas Draycott, QC, Nizam Hosein immediately made seven damaging admissions. He admitted having applied for details of the ownership of the Rolls-Royce, of having placed the paper flowers at the ransom drop-off point, and of having written down the number of the van by which the ransom money was to be placed, among other things. Any chance that the jury might acquit for lack of a body was now gone.

Arthur Hosein could not deny the scientific evidence linking him to the crime. He had been bombastic in the witness box, jeering at the prosecutor and arguing with his brother. When the Attorney-General lost his place in a pile of witness statements, Arthur rebuked him: 'Come on, Mr Attorney-General, you can do better than that.' His arrogance never abandoned him, even at the darkest hour. He told the jury a fantastic story of having seen his brother Nizam in conference with the Mafia at the farm, and was now to be made a scapegoat for their crimes. Under cross-examination, he became almost hysterical with rage.

Alick McKay had attended every day of the trial. On the last day of the three-week trial, 6 October 1970, he heard the jury find the bothers guilty as charged. Arthur Hosein immediately began shouting abuse at the judge, Mr Justice Sebag Shaw, accusing him of racial prejudice, as a Jew trying a Muslim. 'Injustice has not only been done, it has also been seen and heard by the gallery to have been done. They have seen the provocation of your Lordship and your immense partiality . . . it is a grave injustice.'

The brothers were sentenced to life imprisonment, with an additional twenty-five years for Arthur on the kidnapping charge, and fifteen for Nizam. (The jury had recommended mercy in his case.) Sentencing the brothers, the judge said the kidnapping of Muriel McKay and her confinement had been cold-blooded and abominable. 'So long as she remained alive, she was reduced to terrifying despair in a way which has shocked and revolted every right-minded person.' The judge went on to praise Chief Superintendent Smith and his team for a piece of 'brilliant detective work'. (The officers involved held a party at Tiffany's nightclub in Wimbledon to celebrate after the case, even considering the possibility of designing a special tie for all those who had been involved in the McKay inquiry. Two crossed bill-hooks with a crow sitting above them was suggested . . .)

Yet we cannot even be certain that Muriel McKay died at Rooks Farm. Not one single pathologist was ever called to the farm to examine it. And in view of the many stupid acts of the Hosein brothers, the obvious question is why on earth didn't the police catch them sooner?

How did Muriel McKay die? Most likely from sheer cold and exhaustion, with her body then being fed to the pigs. She was fifty-five, and of delicate constitution. It could not be, as the police suggested, that she was killed in fury when the brothers realized they had the wrong women. Inept as they were, the Hoseins knew that they could not bargain with a corpse.

When did Muriel McKay die? Most likely within the first few days, and probably on 1 January 1970. Arthur Hosein's wife and children were due back from holiday a couple of days later. The evidence *had* to be removed before then.

Why did Muriel McKay die? That is easier to answer. Any ransom deal had to be done within the first forty-eight hours. That was not possible for three reasons: Alick McKay could not possibly raise so much cash in so short a time, the Hosein brothers were reluctant to talk about precise details of ransom drops over the phone for a long time, and they had been stupid in failing to leave a ransom demand when they snatched their hostage, which would have made it clear from the outset that it *was* a kidnapping for money.

Arthur Hosein, in particular, thought he was a criminal genius demonstrating his superiority over the police – it was that fatal flaw of arrogance in his character again. In fact, he was such a clumsy criminal that some writers postulate the existence of a third man, the 'mastermind' in the plot, whose existence has never been discovered. I would discount this for one reason: Arthur Hosein's overweening conceit. He would never have kept quiet for so long, in view of the free publicity on offer from newspapers and magazines to feed his ego. Not even large cash offers have persuaded him to tell us what happened to Muriel McKay.

9
IAN SIMMS: THE TRIUMPH OF THE GENETIC FINGERPRINT

In forensic terms, it was the trial of the century. A man was to be tried for murder, yet the prosecution couldn't say how the victim had died because there was no body. All they had were a few circumstantial clues and some blood.

Most kinds of murder do involve the spilling of blood; in this particular instance the blood clinched the case. But if it hadn't been for the brilliant pioneering work of a professor in an obscure English university, the prosecution would have had no hope of securing a conviction. Once again the recently developed technique of the 'genetic fingerprint' was to prove its value, demonstrating beyond reasonable doubt that it is the biggest single advance in the fight against crime since the adoption of actual fingerprinting in 1901.

The mystery began when pretty Helen McCourt, aged twenty-two, vanished from the face of the earth on the afternoon of Tuesday 9 February 1988. Her mother was waiting for her with her tea prepared at home in the village of Billinge, near St Helen's, on Merseyside. But Helen never arrived home.

Helen lived with her mother and father in Standish Avenue, Billinge, a small village where everyone knew everybody else. When her anxious parents reported her disappearance to the police, detectives quickly realized that they were dealing with a possible murder or kidnapping, rather than a routine missing-person report.

They reconstructed Helen's last movements, discovering that she had left the Liverpool Royal Insurance Company, where she worked as a computer operator, at 4 p.m. She had caught the 4.16 p.m. train from Liverpool Lime Street to St Helens.

An office colleague had travelled on the train with her, and they had chatted briefly. Once at St Helen's, Helen had bought cosmetics from a chemist's shop, before catching the bus to Billinge. The driver remembered her getting off at 5.15 p.m. The stop was just three hundred yards from her home. In that short stretch between the bus stop and her home Helen had vanished, and to this day her body has never been found.

The police questioned everyone in the village and came across a woman witness who had heard a scream coming from the direction of the village pub, the George and Dragon, some ten minutes after the bus dropped Helen off. The witness said the scream was 'sharp and fairly high-pitched, and stopped dead'.

The police found this piece of evidence very interesting. They had already been to Helen's office and found her diary, in which the name of the pub and its landlord, thirty-three-year-old Ian Simms, cropped up with some frequency. They made a house-to-house search along the High Street, in which the pub was situated.

While a squad of officers was busy on this task, another team was checking up on Helen's background. It seemed she spent a lot of time at the George and Dragon, staying after hours and drinking into the early morning. Two days before vanishing, Helen had been barred from the pub, following an angry scuffle with another girl. A couple of witnesses said they had heard landlord Ian Simms say that he 'hated' Helen.

Experienced detectives tend not to jump at every clue or suspect like a bull at a gate. The slow and methodical following of established routine remains the key to good detection.

Every house and shop was searched along the High

Street, until eventually officers arrived at the George and Dragon to question Simms. He said he was baffled by Helen's disappearance. More importantly, he had what appeared to be a cast-iron alibi. Married, with two children, Simms also kept a young mistress in the flat above the pub and said he had been with her all evening at the relevant time. Simms' wife and two children lived in a house a few hundred yards from the pub.

So Simms liked the ladies. There was no crime in that, and there was no body hidden away in his flat. A search had revealed nothing except possibly one puzzling detail: gritty sand deposits in the bottom of his bath. But that did not connect him with Helen McCourt's disappearance.

Further questioning of the locals led to fresh information, particularly about Simms. On the day Helen vanished, a woman whose house overlooked the pub had glanced out of her window at about 6 p.m. and noticed Simms moving his car from its usual parking spot in front of the pub to a side gate leading to a bowling green.

Simms said he had not left the pub all night, so was it significant that he had moved his car? Had he moved it to a more secluded spot in order to load a body into its boot? Detective Superintendent Tom Davies, head of the CID at St Helen's, and Detective Inspector George Durno, decided to pay Simms a visit.

Simms had been questioned previously and had appeared to be cool and self-possessed, a man with nothing to hide. Now, shortly after noon on 11 February, he was about to be questioned again, this time by the two senior detectives heading the inquiry.

The officers told him that so far Helen's body had not been found. Was he sure he had not left the pub that evening? When did he last see Helen? Why did he move his car? Where did the sand and grit deposits noted in the bottom of his bath come from?

Simms shrugged and said coolly that they would have

to ask his girlfriend: she had been the last one to take a bath. While asking these simple questions, however, the officers noticed that Simms was getting very nervous. His stomach was visibly pumping as he tried to speak, and he stumbled over his words.

It was enough to alert them, and they decided to take him to the police station for further questioning. He was not under arrest, they assured him, just helping them with their inquiries.

While Simms was at the police station making a statement, detectives took the opportunity to search his car, finding a broken earring in the boot. Its clip was missing, and Helen's mother recognized it as having belonged to her daughter.

Inside the interview room, a detective noticed fine scratches on Simms' face and neck. Simms said he had got them when walking his dog through brambles and nettles. He was again asked to account for his movements on the afternoon and evening of Helen's disappearance, having been told that his girlfriend had broken his alibi. She said he had not arrived at the pub until 10 p.m. Could he account for those vital missing hours?

Simms now changed his story. He said it was true he was late getting back to the pub, but he had been sitting in his car at Southport beach for hours, weeping, distressed about his failing marriage. He had been too ashamed to mention it before.

Mr Davies then showed him the earring recovered from his car and asked: 'What can you tell me about this?'

Simms shook his head. 'Nothing.'

Mr Davies then said: 'I am arresting you on suspicion of the murder of Helen McCourt. This earring has been identified as hers and she was wearing it on Tuesday. How do you account for it being found in the boot of your car?'

Simms replied: 'I have not seen Helen since Sunday. Someone else must have put it in my car.' He was to remain very cool and self-possessed, with a ready excuse for everything. But some things could not be explained away so easily.

His car was still being searched and a forensic scientist found traces of blood in the boot. Detectives armed with a search warrant went back to the flat above the pub again, and this time they looked more carefully.

They found the missing earring clip in the bedroom. Tiny tufts of human hair were found by the bed, some of them torn out by the roots. Blood was found on a pair of Simms' jeans and a sweatshirt. More blood was found on the floor and stairs. Tests showed it to be of human origin. If Helen had been murdered, then it seemed probable that she had met her end in the flat above the pub, and her body was transported somewhere in the boot of Simms's car.

Simms' young mistress was now questioned and told police about the scratch marks she had noticed on his neck on the night Helen vanished. Simms had explained them away by saying that they had been caused by his wife Nadine, who had attacked him after finding out about his affair. But when the wife was questioned, she said she *hadn't known* about any affair until the police told her . . .

The pub staff were interviewed, and told police that they had seen Simms cleaning the floor of his flat with bleach, giving the excuse that his dog had made a mess. They had also noticed that a lot of plastic bin-liners were missing from the cleaner's cupboard.

The police now had a mass of circumstantial evidence, and some blood, but it was all very nebulous. It is one thing to have blood samples, but you have to have a body from which to take other blood samples to be certain they match. Or, at least, that *used* to be the case, before Professor Alec Jeffrey discovered the genetic fingerprint test at Leicester University – a test used in an historic 'first' to convict Colin Pitchfork in 1987 of the murder of two schoolgirls.

The secret of the genetic fingerprint lies in the fact that every individual is made up of some hundred million million cells, each of which contains forty-six chromosomes, twenty-three of which come from the father's sperm, the other twenty-three from the mother's egg. This basic biological principle had been known as long ago as 1911. It took longer to discover that chromosomes are made up of the DNA material, the building-blocks of life.

What Alec Jeffrey did was to devise a method of testing the profile or code of DNA material present in a person's body fluids – sperm, blood, saliva – and even in the roots of hair, and producing from this a 'print' unique to the individual. No two people on this planet – save identical twins – can have the same genetic 'autograph'. And the genetic 'code' in this print should show characteristics from both the mother and the father. In fact, the test was first used in disputed paternity cases.

In this case, forensic scientists came up with a bright idea. They had blood on Simms' clothing, which they suspected had come from Helen. But they did not have Helen's body. However, by taking samples from her mother and father, they could carry out a DNA genetic fingerprint test to determine if the blood came from an offspring of the parents. If it did, it would show a relationship because of those chromosomes from both parents. If successful, it would be the first conviction 'by proxy' using the DNA test.

The DNA test was carried out on both parents and their profile established. Then the blood from Simms' clothing was tested, its profile being matched against that from the parents. The test result was a positive conclusion that the blood found on Simms' jeans was 126,000 times more likely to have come from an offspring of Mr and Mrs McCourt than from a random member of the population. The codes matched.

Despite all the evidence presented to him, Simms never cracked. He maintained that the incriminating items found in his car and flat had been planted by some unknown enemy. And as for the suggestion of murder, his stock reply was: 'Show me the body.' He was a very cool customer indeed.

Even after an intensive police search for miles around, Helen's body had still not been found, nor any clue as to its fate. Then, three weeks after she disappeared, and with Simms in custody, a fitness instructor out for a run found her handbag on the bank of the River Irwell, fifteen miles from Billinge.

Police combed the area, and found most of Helen's clothing and possessions in a black plastic bin-liner near the river. A man walking his dog three miles away found a man's bloodstained clothing dumped on a slag-heap. That clothing proved to belong to Ian Simms.

Simms was to spend a year in prison awaiting trial for the murder, and the police made the most of that year, tying up loose ends and tracing potential new witnesses. It was the first ever murder trial to go ahead on Merseyside without a body, and the decision to prosecute Simms might have seemed a brave one, because the Crown Prosecution Service guidelines are not to initiate a prosecution without more than a fifty per cent chance of a conviction, and they always knew that a conviction was going to be difficult. Juries tend to be hard-headed people who want absolute proof. They too might say: 'Show us the body.' Without a body, it is impossible to establish a motive or determine whether the crime was rape, robbery or revenge.

For the whole of that year the flat above the pub had been sealed by the police. They left nothing to chance. The forensic clues were to lie undisturbed.

The trial of Ian Simms began at Liverpool Crown Court on Tuesday, 21 February 1989. Reporters from all over the country were packed into the courtroom to listen to this unique case.

Mr Brian Leveson, QC, prosecuting, began by relating the mysterious circumstances surrounding Helen

McCourt's disappearance. Telling of how she stepped off a bus just three hundred yards from her home, Mr Leveson said bleakly: 'Helen McCourt never made it home. She has never been seen or heard of since, and has never been found, alive or dead.'

Mr Leveson then made the bold claim that forensic science would 'prove beyond all doubt' that Ian Simms had murdered her. He mentioned the technique of DNA fingerprinting. Helen had never been a blood donor, so her blood group was not known. However, scientists had taken blood samples from her parents and matched it against the blood found on Simms' clothing.

He told the jury that there was other evidence against Simms: his fingerprint in blood found at the bottom of the pub stairs; the earring and blood found in his car; his clothing found three miles from where Helen's clothing and possessions had been dumped.

Telling of Helen's last known movements, Mr Leveson said: 'The Crown alleges that she has been murdered and her body hidden so well that it has not been found, although a very considerable effort has been put into looking for it.'

He also revealed that nearly all of Helen's clothing and possessions had been recovered from sites at Hollins Green and Irlam. An opal and sapphire earring she was wearing on the day she vanished was subsequently found in the boot of Simms' car. The butterfly clip which fitted it had been found in a rear bedroom in his flat at the pub. Mr Leveson claimed that Simms had gone to bed with his young mistress at the pub within hours of killing Helen, as if nothing was amiss.

Mr Leveson explained that a peculiar pale-coloured mud had been found on a bracelet and two rings Simms had been wearing when he was arrested. Simms said he had spent the evening that Helen disappeared at Southport beach, but the mud did not come from that locality. It would, no doubt, be the defence suggestion that someone else had planted incriminating items on Simms to fabricate evidence against him, but the jewellery told a very different story.

'This is not a case of somebody else wearing Ian Simms' clothing and jewellery. One of the rings would not even come off. This undeniably and incontrovertibly involves Ian Simms himself.'

Mr Leveson said that the colour of the mud found on the bracelet and rings (one of the rings had to be removed by a doctor) was very similar to that found on Simms' clothing and inside his car. 'Simms had at least been up to his wrists in pale mud,' Mr Leveson said, adding that the wealth of circumstantial and forensic evidence meant that the scientists alone were making the case absolutely overwhelming against Simms.

It was, however, the task of the prosecution to prove four things: that Helen McCourt was dead; that her attacker intended to kill her, or at the very least to cause her serious bodily harm; that she died as a result of violence inflicted upon her without any lawful excuse; and finally, that Simms was the attacker. Put like that, and without a body, it seemed a daunting task.

It had already been overwhelmingly proved that Helen had indeed been attacked, Mr Leveson said, and a number of features indicated the clearest intent of the attacker to inflict really serious bodily harm. There were blood splashes at the foot of the stairs leading up to Simms' flat. Unless the first blow is of tremendous ferocity, Mr Leveson explained, blood splashing occurs when part of the body already bloody is hit again.

On the first day of the trial the judge, jury and Ian Simms were taken to the pub where the alleged murder took place. The party spent an hour and a half inside, before a pale and withdrawn Simms emerged, ignoring the huge crowd of neighbours and reporters who had gathered outside. Simms was handcuffed to police officers, and blinked nervously in the bright sunlight.

Helen's mother went into the witness box on the second day of the trial. She identified items belonging to her daughter which had been recovered by the police, including an address book. Taking frequent sips of water, she identified in turn a red comb, a wooden key-ring with keys attached, a pearl-coloured hair slide and a circular purse. She also identified objects which she would have expected to find among Helen's belongings, including luncheon vouchers, jewellery and items of clothing. There was also a half-read paperback novel, three crossword puzzles, a shampoo, body lotion, nail varnish and lipstick.

She broke down in tears only once, when she was shown the brown coat Helen had been wearing. She recovered her composure, steeling herself for the ordeal, and then went on with the grim task of identifying the rest of her daughter's possessions.

Giving her evidence in a low monotone, Mrs McCourt said that after Helen had disappeared, a policewoman dressed in similar clothing had walked her last known movements in a reconstruction designed to jog people's memories. This had taken place only a few days after Helen vanished, and weeks before the items she had identified had been recovered by the police.

Cross-examined by Mr John Kay, QC, Mrs McCourt said that she and Helen's grandmother had been due to meet Helen in Liverpool on the day she disappeared, but the meeting had been cancelled because of bad weather. She said that Helen had three identical earrings, because she had lost one and bought a replacement pair.

The mother agreed that Helen's behaviour had changed after her former boyfriend broke off their relationship of two and a half years the previous September. Helen had been very upset and had started staying out late and drinking.

On one occasion, in September 1987, Helen had stayed out all night, not returning home until eight o'clock in the morning. The entry in Helen's diary for that date confirmed that she had spent the night at the George and Dragon. There was a further reference in the diary to a night when Helen stayed out until 4 a.m. The inference was that Helen and Simms had been lovers.

Replying to a question from defence counsel, Mrs McCourt said that Helen had not mentioned to her anything about a scuffle with another girl in the pub, or about being banned from the George and Dragon. Neither had she noticed any scratches or grazes on her daughter's arm.

An office colleague of Helen's testified that she and Helen had spent their coffee break together shortly before Helen left work for the last time, and she had been amazed when Helen showed her a long scratch on the back of her left hand. Helen said that it was caused by a fingernail or ring during a fight with another girl, although Helen was not the sort of person to get involved in a fight. She identified the clothing Helen had been wearing on her last day alive.

It was on the fourth day of the trial that Simms' girlfriend went into the witness box to tell of her relationship with him. She said she had been eighteen when she first started having sex with him, towards the end of 1986. By the middle of 1987, she had started sleeping at the pub. At first she stayed one night a week, but by Christmas 1987 this had increased to a couple of nights a week and all weekend. Simms was sleeping permanently at the pub, telling his wife it was for 'security' reasons.

In January 1988 she had moved in permanently at the pub, but when her mother complained, her overnight stays became limited to weekends and the odd week night. The girl said that she and Simms had gone on holiday together to Tenerife and also stayed at top hotels in Britain. She had once asked Simms if his wife knew about them. He had replied that she didn't, but probably suspected something. She finished her evidence by blurting out to the jury: 'I loved him – and I still do!' Then she burst into tears.

After composing herself, she was ready to face cross-examination. Simms's young girlfriend said that she had often seen Helen McCourt at the pub. There were always a few 'stay behinds' and Helen was usually one of them. She had last seen Helen on the Friday night, chatting to a barman – four days before she vanished.

A couple of days later she had heard that there had been an argument in the pub between Helen and another girl over a photograph of a man, and Simms had had to split them up.

Turning to the night of the alleged murder, the girlfriend said that she usually went to the pub at seven p.m. each evening, but that day Simms had telephoned her at about six fifteen, asking her not to come until eight-thirty. When she asked why, he had just said: 'Nadine.'

The girl said that when she got to the pub Simms wasn't there, so she sat on the bed in the flat watching TV until he came in at about 10 p.m. He explained his lateness by saying that Nadine, his wife, had found out about their affair and had 'gone berserk'. He pointed to his neck and said: 'Look what she has done.' She saw two faint red marks about a couple of inches long, but they were not bleeding. Simms sent her down to look after the bar while he had a bath.

When she went back up to the flat at ten-thirty, Simms told her that he had been home to confess his affair to his wife, hoping to seek some solution, but she had become angry and upset, so he had left.

The witness first heard about Helen's disappearance on 10 February. She had gone to the pub and found Simms working on his account books. They talked about Helen being missing and Simms said he had spent the previous evening on Southport beach, feeling upset over the row with his wife. Then the witness and Simms went to bed. The next day, at noon, she got a phone call from Simms asking her if she could look after the pub while he went to the police station to be interviewed.

There was a weekend break in the trial, which recommenced on the Monday with the youngest sister of Simms' girlfriend telling the jury: 'Ian Simms really did not like Helen McCourt because of the way she was with him.'

Another female witness said that after Simms had thrown Helen out of the pub, he told his customers he hated her. The witness found this strange, as Helen was 'very happy and outgoing. She was a very nice friend and very pretty'.

The retired baker who had found Simms' bloodstained clothing was the next witness. He said he had lived in the Hollins Green area of Manchester for thirty years, and regularly took his dog for a walk over the local steelworks slagheap tip.

At 7.30 a.m. on 10 February the previous year, he had noticed a car close to the canal bank. A few minutes later he had come across clothing on the towpath. There were two boots, and a towel covered in blood. There was also a pair of jeans on a nearby bank.

'The jeans were concertinaed as if someone had just stepped out of them. They were muddy and the clay was wet. I put my hands over the top of them by the crotch and it seemed warm to me. None of the clothing was wet. I have a sensitive touch – most bakers do – and I could feel the warmth of the jeans. I thought to myself that they had been dumped there a few minutes before I arrived.'

He had later discussed his find with his wife and as a result informed the police at about 10 a.m.

Two of Helen's uncles told of going to the pub and questioning Simms about Helen's disappearance. They wanted to test his reactions and claimed that he had been 'fidgety and ill-at-ease'. To test if he was telling the truth, they had asked him a few simple questions to which they already knew the answers.

'Did Helen spend much time in the pub?' and 'Did she ever stay behind?' Simms had answered no to both questions, convicting him as a liar in their minds.

Police surgeon Dr Miles Clark told of examining Simms after his arrest. He had carried out the two-and-a-half-hour examination in the early hours of 12 February, and found numerous fine scratches on Simms's body, legs and arms. Some of the scratches were consistent with having been caused by fingernails, others by vegetation.

Simms at first said that the scratches were caused by the girl involved in the fight with Helen in the pub, but later said they had been caused by walking through brambles.

The fitness instructor who had found Helen's clothing and other possessions said he had seen an open handbag by the River Irwell. There were a few items of cosmetics nearby. He put the make-up in the handbag, which contained a diary and credit cards, but no money, and took the bag home. He thought it had been stolen from a car, them dumped. Once home, he examined the bag more carefully and saw a card bearing the name 'Helen McCourt'. He recognized it as being the name of the missing girl and notified the police. He took police back to the site, where a further search had recovered more items.

Detective Sergeant Kevin Conroy testified on the ninth day of the trial, saying that when he confronted Simms with the fact that his bloodstained clothing had been found, Simms had immediately retorted that it had been 'planted' and said that other incriminating evidence had been fabricated by someone with a grudge against him.

He maintained that the scratches on his neck were caused by the girl he ejected from the pub. Told that his girlfriend had not seen those scratches prior to Helen's disappearance, Simms said he had covered the scratches with make-up because his girlfriend was 'the jealous type'.

When shown the clothing, Simms refused to recognize it as being his. Later he said: 'I have felt in recent weeks that someone has been in the flat with their own set of keys.' He said that someone could have taken his clothing from the flat and driven his car away. Six other people had keys to his car and he had not used it himself on the night that Helen vanished. If it had been at Hollins Green at that time, then someone else must have been driving it.

Simms insisted that if he had committed the murder he would have set fire to the car and all the incriminating evidence, then claimed that it had been stolen. After fourteen hours of questioning, Simms had ended with the pious hope that Helen's body would soon be found so that the forensic scientists could prove he had nothing to do with killing her.

One police witness agreed with a defence suggestion that Simms's nervous reaction under questioning might have been due to the fact that his illicit affair was not going to remain secret much longer.

During the third week of the trial the jury were taken at their own request to the site where Simms' clothing had been found. The jury spent twenty minutes examining the scene, while in the background Simms stood laughing and joking with his warders.

On 7 March Home Office forensic scientist Dr John Moore told the court about the blood and mud he had found in Simms' car. He had also found blood on the carpet in the rear bedroom above the pub, and on the stair carpet. He had examined Simms' car on 11 February the previous year. As well as bright yellow mud on the offside, there was some in the footwells, on the pedals, driver's seat, steering wheel, gear lever and fascia.

'There were also four adjacent smears on the top of the driver's door. In my opinion these were consistent with having been made by mud-stained fingers.'

He had also found blood on the carpet in the boot, and beneath the carpet a broken earring. He had later gone back to the pub and concentrated on the stairs leading to the flat and the landing. 'I found a spot of blood on the fifth tread of the stairs from the top. It was a circular spot about six-tenths of an inch in diameter.'

He had gone to the pub again on 18 March and examined the rear bedroom. 'Between the bed and a chest of drawers I saw several human head hairs on the carpet, and near to them was a bloodstain. It was a smear of blood about two and a half inches long by half an inch wide.'

The following day Simms himself went into the witness box, hoping to dispel some of the suspicion attaching to him. He told the jury (in an attempt to account for Helen's hair in his bedroom) that he had once gone to bed with her. He said he and Helen kissed and cuddled, but it had gone no further than that.

He said that Helen often stayed behind after hours and usually visited the pub four or five times a week. They were friends, he said, claiming: 'Helen used to confide in me and I would tell her about my circumstances, and we would both laugh about it.'

Questioned by his defence counsel, Simms said that the fingerprints in blood found on the door at the bottom of the stairs leading to the flat above had been there for two months prior to Helen's disappearance. He said a lot of people had been cut in the pub, particularly one man on New Year's Eve. He had taken this man upstairs to bandage his wound. This was how his own fingerprints in blood had come to be deposited. He did not know the man's name . . .

He also told the jury that he had never been to the site at Irlam where his jacket and Helen's belongings had been found. He admitted that it was his jacket but said that he had not worn it for a long time. Neither had he ever seen the spade recovered from the river, although the previous pub landlord had testified that he had left it behind at the pub when he moved out.

He said he never washed his car, and mud had got on to it when he took his dog out to the countryside. The last time was on 8 February, the previous year, when he got mud all over his waders, which he had then put into the boot of his car.

Looking directly at the jury, Simms told them: 'I have not seen her since the Monday night. I have never set eyes on her. I never touched her.' He concurred that the clothing found at Hollins Green 'probably did' belong to him, but must have been taken from his flat by a mystery man.

Mr Leveson, in cross-examination, asked: 'Would you agree that you have perfected the art of lying so that you can do it not only with ease and skill, but also most successfully?'

Simms was forced to admit that he had told lies to his family, friends and the police. He agreed that keeping an illicit affair secret from his wife was 'living a lie'.

Asked to explain the discrepancies in his initial statements to the police, Simms said they were due to 'numerous detectives who bamboozled me with questions, and tried to twist my words'. He claimed that the police officers involved had told lies. Then Mr Leveson asked him why detectives involved in the case should lie. Simms said they might have done so for professional reasons, because they had made their minds up that he was involved in Helen McCourt's disappearance.

Simms denied ever banning Helen from the pub, or having said that he hated her. When reminded that a witness had testified that he didn't really like Helen, Simms said that it was a mistaken impression. He said the police account of interviews with him was not a fair summary.

Mr Leveson asked Simms why a knot in his electrical flex, which was found with Helen's clothes, contained hairs matching hers. Simms said that he thought someone had managed to get the flex and put her hair in the knot.

Mr Justice Caulfield asked Simms if he thought it was to 'fix him up'.

Simms replied: 'Yes, in fact I know they did.'

The judge asked Simms to explain why his grey blood-stained jacket had been found with Helen's things, weeks after she disappeared.

Simms replied: 'I haven't got a clue. If I had done anything, I wouldn't have left it with her clothes, would I?'

After thirteen days of evidence – and on his birthday – Simms listened as prosecuting counsel urged the jury to convict him. Mr Leveson began by asking the jury to consider the events chronologically, and went through the case again, step by step.

Mr Leveson said that a touchstone against which to start judging Simms' evidence 'is that Simms says the police got together and concocted an entirely false account of events at the pub. An easy way to test whether Simms was lying, or the police, is to consider the fact that Simms has a friendly witness who feels very strongly about him, but who is not prepared to lie – his girlfriend. Her version of the events at the pub on the night Helen disappeared is consistent with the police account.'

Mr Leveson went on: 'Simms claims he has been bamboozled, sworn at and deprived of a lawyer when he was interviewed as only a witness. He now says he did not make mistakes in that statement: he had been lying. He said the police at that time were simply trying to take a witness statement from him, but Helen's earring was then found in the boot of his car, along with blood, and he was again questioned about his quite ludicrous account.

'Then the police had some luck – and that is what it was, absolute luck – because while all this was going on something else had happened. A witness walking his dog had found some warm clothing which looked as if someone had just stepped out of it. Simms said he would not have left his stuff there if he'd intended to hide it – of course not. He was nearly caught!

'At the same time, seventeen miles away outside the

George and Dragon, a young man was waiting for his father to give him a lift *and Simms' car was not there*.'

Mr Leveson referred to the items found at Irlam, including items bought at a chemist's shop. 'The cashier at the chemist's was asked to identify the items from the receipt, and she found a 49p item missing. And so the police were ordered back to search the place again, and found this toothbrush.'

'As a result, an earring butterfly clip was found. It was an enormous irony that if the cashier had identified stockings found at Irlam as the 49p item, this further search would not have taken place and the clip, hair and bloodstains would not have been found.'

Tackling Simms' allegations that he had been framed, Mr Leveson said: 'The "real" murderer would have had to get into his pub and carry out the murder without alerting Simms' dog. Like the dog in the Sherlock Holmes story "The Silver Blaze", the dog did not bark. *It remained silent because it knew the murderer*.'

Mr Leveson commended the thoroughness of the police investigation, saying that the jury could be sure that Helen was dead. 'She would have come forward if she was still alive. The evidence is that Simms killed her. Why did she die? We do not know. Was there some row? We do not know. Only two people can tell us; one of them is dead. The Crown submits to you that you can have absolutely no doubt at all that the other is now sitting in the dock.'

Mr Kay, QC, got up to make the closing speech for the defence. He urged the jury to look closely at the evidence, particularly the forensic evidence, with extreme caution. 'We submit that if you look at the totality of the evidence, there are features which make one say in all probability someone has deliberately tried to make it look as if Ian Simms is responsible.'

Mr Kay said that witnesses were mistaken about seeing lights blazing at the pub on the two mornings following the alleged murder, when Simms was allegedly getting rid of Helen's body and belongings. 'If Simms was there, he would have been foolish to put all the lights on at the front. I have no doubt you will disapprove of Simms having a girlfriend and a wife, but sadly, it is not an uncommon situation.

'In some ways Simms could be considered the sort of man who would commit murder. It is the knowledge that others will disapprove which causes people to tell lies in matters of this kind . . . In hours of taped interviews he has never said anything which could be interpreted as an admission of guilt. Without the clothing, there is not the beginning of a conclusive case against this defendant. The Crown says he parked his car at Hollins Green and walked along a pathway, where he stripped naked. But if he was there in the car, there was a canal right alongside it into which he could have thrown the clothes and been back within seconds. The Crown say he did not have time to hide the clothing, and for some reason stripped off in the middle of this pathway. The prosecution say this man has been the clever person responsible for this operation. Yet they say this same man dropped clothing in the middle of the pathway. If it was the defendant, and he decided to put his clothes in one place and Helen's in another, he could not leave his jacket with her clothing.'

'Did the police have the absolute luck, or is it that someone was making sure the police did have the good fortune and luck?'

In his summing-up, the judge said that if Simms had killed Helen McCourt, he was in the first division of cold-blooded murderers. 'If Ian Simms is guilty of murder, he had no respect for the corpse. Those who loved Helen were denied the tribute they could have paid to her . . . What remains of Helen McCourt? Just a few strands of hair – but you may think eventually important strands of hair . . .

'If Simms killed Helen McCourt, he still retained

enough passion for himself to make love to his young mistress. If he murdered Helen McCourt, he showed cunning, did he not, in the disposal of her garments and the disposal of his garments? That is, if the prosecution are correct. I have placed emphasis on the "if". You have to decide whether the Crown have proved that Simms committed the murder; whether Helen is dead; that Simms unlawfully killed her; and that he had in his mind the intent to kill Helen or to cause her serious bodily harm. If ever there was a case where every iota of evidence has to be considered, this case is it. There has not been a body for pathologists to examine. It is a heavy responsibility, but I urge you to reach a unanimous verdict.'

The judge, in dealing with the mass of evidence, reminded the jury that Helen had been given a pair of emerald-green mittens by a friend. A scientist had told the court that a single fibre said to be exactly similar to the green mittens was found on Simms' jacket.

On Tuesday, 14 March 1989, the jury of seven women and five men retired, taking five and a half hours to find Simms guilty of murder. Sentencing him to life imprisonment, the judge told Simms: 'After grave and long deliberation, the jury has said you took the life of this young, happy girl, and that you have hidden or desecrated her body so her parents can never respect her corpse. You have cast her garments virtually to the rats. You have done this coldly and callously and shown no remorse.'

Simms was hustled from the dock shouting: 'I've never seen the girl!' There was uproar in the court, Helen's friends and relatives shouting abuse, and others cheering the verdict.

The judge said sternly: 'Is there no respect for this court? I know your grief and horror and anguish, but you must remain quiet.' He then praised the 'brilliant police work', saying: 'I commend the fantastic care they have executed in this case.'

The verdict was an historic legal 'first' – the first murder conviction achieved with genetic fingerprinting 'by proxy'.

Outside the court, Mrs McCourt pleaded brokenly: 'I just hope he tells us where Helen's body is now. He is going down for life. Maybe he will now open his mouth to end our agony.' Detectives involved in the case have vowed never to rest until they have found Helen's body.

The reason why Simms killed Helen will never be known. It was not a particularly clever murder, and the only reason it echoes in the mind is that he was fiendishly lucky in hiding the body so well. It lies somewhere still in a makeshift grave.

It is always difficult to convict for murder without a body. The evidence has to be overwhelming; enough to satisfy a scientist. The first scientist of whom we have record is St Thomas. The Bible records that he said of the Resurrection: 'Except I shall see in His hands the print of the nails, and put my finger into the print of the nails, and thrust my hand into His side, I will not believe.' (John 20:25). In this case the Doubting Thomases were offered an array of scientific evidence sufficient to convince anyone.

And in all such cases, it is those who read the evidence who become the final judges . . .

10
THE JEALOUS HUSBAND WHO INCINERATED HIS WIFE

Only a handful of all killers attempt to dispose of the bodies of their victims; most leave them where they fall. For that handful, the most common method is to bury the corpse – but bodies have a habit of surfacing. Dropping the corpse into a deep lake has been tried a few times, but inquisitive scuba-divers tend to find them. Haigh used acid. Some use fire, but merely setting fire to the body will not destroy all traces of identity. Teeth can survive burning. To totally destroy the body by fire, something like a furnace is necessary, or even an incinerator, such as Dr Marcel Petiot used for his refugee victims.

Martin James Ryan, a twenty-eight-year-old hospital porter, suspected that his wife was cheating on him. More importantly, he had access to the huge incinerator in the hospital where he worked.

Ryan lived in Barry, South Wales, with his wife Linda. Although ten years older than him, she was an attractive blonde to whom men seemed naturally to flock. What prompted her murder is that Ryan saw her in a Barry public house with two men, and a furious row resulted. Ryan claimed she taunted him about his sexual inadequacy. Whatever was said, the result was that in a cold rage Ryan stabbed his wife to death on the night of 28 June 1990.

He had driven her to the incinerator unit at the hospital and forced her into a chair before stabbing her.

Afterwards he thrust her head-first into the incinerator. Nurses on duty complained of a terrible smell that night, but Ryan fobbed them off with excuses. He hoped he had committed the perfect murder . . .

After the killing, Ryan tried to cover the disappearance of his wife by phoning the shop where she worked, assuming a woman's voice to tell staff there that she wouldn't be able to come to work that day as she had the flu. Two hours later he rang again, this time using his normal voice, to complain that his wife had run out on him and ask if they knew where she was.

He even concocted a love-letter to his wife, written and dated after the murder. But when detectives got suspicious, Ryan panicked and went on the run for a month, living and working in London. When arrested there, he jumped seventy feet from a bathroom window and broke a leg. Even so he made good his escape. When he did arrive back in Barry it was of his own volition. Along with a solicitor, he went to the police station and made a statement confessing to killing his wife. That confession was to be the main substance of the charge against him at his trial for murder.

The trial began at Cardiff Crown Court on 22 April 1991 before Mr Justice Simon Browne. Ryan pleaded not guilty to the charge of murdering his wife. He was hoping for a manslaughter verdict.

Mr John Rees, prosecuting, began by saying that although the body of thirty-eight-year-old Mrs Ryan had never been found, the prosecution would prove that Ryan had murdered her and destroyed her body in an incinerator, probably opening the incinerator valves to increase the temperature and ensure complete cremation.

Mr Rees said that Ryan was a porter at Cardiff's Llandough Hospital. On the evening of 28 June 1990, he saw his wife in a Barry public house with her lover, Mr James Fraser. A violent row ensued, during which Ryan slapped his wife's face. At midnight the same night Ryan drove his wife to the hospital, took her down into the incinerator room, and stabbed her with an eight-inch kitchen knife.

Mr Rees said that neighbours living close to the hospital called the police after hearing two horrifying screams just after midnight. Staff in the maternity wing later complained of a strange smell coming through the air vents. Police who arrived in response to the phone calls found nothing suspicious. But then, they had no reason to look in the incinerator . . .

Mr Rees said: 'This is a case where a body has never been found. The Crown says that the defendant disposed of it in the incinerator at the hospital during the course of a planned and callous killing.'

Describing how a row had led to the murder, Mr Rees went on: 'This is a plain case of murder. He took her there knowing that he was intending to kill her by putting her in the incinerator, not knowing or caring whether she was alive or dead when he did so.' It was this suggestion that Mrs Ryan might have been burned alive that was so horrifying.

Mr Rees then described Ryan's attempts after the murder to conceal the fact of his wife's disappearance by writing a phoney love-letter to her and making those fake phone calls. He had also lied to friends and the police about his wife's whereabouts, and those lies were to the effect that his wife had left him.

Part of Ryan's confession was read to the court. It revealed that shortly before she was murdered and pushed into the incinerator, shop assistant Linda Ryan had told her husband that she didn't love him any more and wished she had never married him.

Ryan had not acted from mad passion or a sudden derangement of the mind. He had told the police that he went 'a bit mad, not violent mad' after being told by his wife that she didn't love him. This admission ruled out any possible insanity plea, or even the possibility of a manslaughter verdict on the grounds of diminished responsibility.

The prosecution disclosed that within a week of killing his wife, Ryan had taken another woman back to his home and spent the night with her in the bed he had shared with his wife. This in itself aroused suspicion among neighbours. When Ryan was questioned closely by the police about his wife's vanishing act, he told lies. Afterwards he panicked and went on the run for a month, travelling first to Manchester, and then on to London, where he booked into the Warwick Court Hotel and got a job in a London public house.

On 19 July three detectives went to that address to question Ryan. He said he would voluntarily go back to Barry with them to assist them with their inquiries, but suddenly ran upstairs and locked himself in a bathroom. The detectives forced open the door, and found no trace of Ryan but simply an open window. Looking out, they saw Ryan lying on the ground, his leg fractured.

Even then he managed to hobble away and make good his escape, making his way to St Mary's Hospital, Paddington, where he was admitted under the name of Paul Adams. While there a nurse happened to spot a tattoo on his arm bearing the name 'Linda'. When she asked who the girl was, Ryan replied: 'Oh, she's no one.' Because for him she had ceased to exist.

He underwent an operation and was subsequently discharged from hospital in August, but found himself with no money and nowhere to stay. He returned to Wales, staying first with his mother in Cardiff, before summoning up the nerve to return to Barry. He went to see a solicitor, who accompanied him to Barry police station on 8 August. He was questioned by detectives and immediately replied: 'I wasn't myself. I have killed my wife.'

During an interview he told detectives that his marriage had been bad for about eighteen months, due to his wife's excessive drinking. On the night of 28 June she had promised to come straight home from work, but never arrived. He went looking for her and saw her with two men in the Windsor public house.

Later, he drove her to the incinerator unit; 'I just wanted a chat,' he explained. Once inside the building he grabbed his wife and thrust her into a chair. They exchanged angry words and she told him: 'I don't love you any more. I wish I'd never married you. I prefer to be with my friends in the pub.'

Ryan then went out to his car, got a knife, and returned with it, stabbing his wife once in the breast as she sat in the chair. He denied that his wife had screamed, saying she had just slumped back in the chair 'making a heavy breathing noise'.

Mr Michael Batt, a drinking friend of Ryan's during 1989, gave evidence as a prosecution witness. He said that Ryan had boasted of being able to dispose of a body in the hospital incinerator *a full year before he actually did so.* 'He said he could dispose of a person if he wanted to get rid of them.' In cross-examination he said he didn't know if Ryan was being serious or not when he made the claim.

Another witness told of hearing screams from the area of the hospital on the night of the murder. Mr Martin Joseph said that the screams were those of a woman. 'It was a scream of fear, a scream of someone very, very frightened,' he said.

He described how he had looked through his window, which overlooked the rear of the hospital, when he heard the scream. 'I then heard a man's voice restraining someone, telling them to be quiet or shut up.' After a couple of minutes he heard another scream and then telephoned the police.

Mrs Ryan's lover testified that he had first met her in a public house, and by June the relationship had developed into a sexual one. On the night of 28 June he saw Mrs Ryan in the Windsor public house. Her husband came in at about 9.30 and began shouting at her, slapping her face and knocking glasses off the table.

'He seemed to be in a seething temper but self-controlled,' Mr Fraser said. 'He bade everyone goodnight and left with a nod of acknowledgement, taking Mrs Ryan with him.' It was the last time Mr Fraser ever saw her.

A hospital colleague of Ryan's told the court that Ryan had told him, a week after the alleged murder, that his wife had left him and he was glad about it. Mr Vivian Jones was the boilerman at the hospital and had spoken to Ryan on Friday, 6 July. They had discussed Ryan's missing wife. When he asked Ryan how he felt about his wife leaving him, Ryan said he was 'glad to see the back of her'. The witness added: 'He was not agitated but was his normal self.'

Another witness, a friend of Ryan's, said he had seen Ryan on the night of 28 June very upset and drunk and threatening to kill himself because his wife had left him for another man. The witness tried to calm his down but Ryan jumped into his car and drove off.

A spokesman for the company which manufactured the incinerator testified that at high temperature a body would incinerate in one hour and ten minutes. About two kilograms (4 1/2 lbs) of ash would remain. The incinerator was more than capable of cremating an adult body, he added.

Detective Inspector Gareth Tinnuche told the court about an interview which he had with Ryan at the police station on 10 August. Ryan had said: 'I just snapped and did what I did. I didn't mean to kill her.' Asked why, if he had not intended to kill his wife, he had made no effort to revive her or seek help from the medical staff at the hospital, he replied: 'She was dead.' He said he didn't know how long it took her to die.

Ryan said he had stabbed his wife at the top left side of her chest. He told the detective he couldn't take any more from his wife. He had not planned the crime or decided to do anything to her – 'but it just happened'.

The officer said that Ryan then went on: 'She kept saying she didn't love me any more. I just got into a temper, that's all . . .' Once he had done the deed, he didn't know what to do.

At the end of the interview he was asked if there was anything he wanted to add, and Ryan said simply: 'I loved her.'

At the end of the first week of the trial, Ryan went into the witness box to deny the prosecution claim that he had 'calmly and coolly' disposed of the evidence of his crime by burning his wife's body in the incinerator, or that the crime had been premeditated.

He admitted stabbing his wife to death after she told him: 'I hate you. I want to be with my friends.' After stabbing her, he said, he was crying and frightened, unaware of what to do. Some hours later he opened the door of the incinerator and put his wife's body into it head-first. 'It was panic, that's the truth,' he said.

He hadn't meant to kill her, he said, adding: 'I'm sorry. I really am. You can't get her, obviously, but I would if I could.' It was a curious remark, but by such banalities is murder recalled.

Under cross-examination he denied being petrified of going to prison for murder – 'which is why you have told this jury lie after lie'.

He agreed that in the past he had used words to his wife similar to: 'If you ever leave me I will kill you.'

Mr Rees asked: 'You decided the marriage was over and you decided cold-bloodedly to kill your wife?'

Ryan replied: 'You are wrong there.'

When asked if he had treated his wife like a possession, Ryan replied defensively: 'She was my wife, after all.'

Ryan denied that his wife had at any time attempted to escape from the incinerator unit or screamed for help. He said he had put the knife into her only once, and agreed that he had not gone into a frenzy and stabbed her repeatedly.

Mr Rees asked him: 'What really went on at the incinerator house? What really happened?'

Ryan replied: 'We just had an argument and it just got

out of hand and I stabbed my wife. I didn't mean to do it.'

'Why didn't you get a doctor from the hospital to see if there was any chance of saving her, if you didn't mean for her to die?'

'Because there was no life there. I was frightened.' He added that he had 'gone to pieces'.

Mr Rees asked him if he had experienced any remorse afterwards. 'Did you cradle her in your arms, crying and kissing her?'

Ryan said he did. He said it was not true that he had calmly and coolly disposed of his wife's body, the only evidence against him, and denied opening the valves of the incinerator and feeding hospital waste on to his wife's body.

He agreed that at no time before his wife's disappearance did he receive treatment from a doctor because of the breakdown of his marriage. He wasn't treated for anxiety, depression, loss of sleep or work. 'I got my problems out of the way without seeing a doctor,' he said bluntly. But he had got his problems out of the way by resorting to murder . . .

Dr Charles Hunt, a forensic psychiatrist, was called as an expert witness for the Crown. He said that Ryan was not suffering from any abnormality of the mind which would have substantially impaired his responsibility for the killing. He had interviewed Ryan for two hours in April and had concluded that he was not a neurotic and vulnerable personality. Ryan specifically denied ever striking his wife – despite evidence that he had hit her and another woman in his past. There was no evidence that he was shy or withdrawn.

To counter this, Dr Sidney Nam, a psychiatrist, was called for the defence. He said that Ryan *was* suffering from an abnormality of the mind and had an anxiety depressive neurosis. He was highly strung, an excessive worrier, had poor self-confidence and was sensitive to criticism. At the time of the killing, in his opinion, Ryan would have been severely depressed and agitated.

Cross-examined by the prosecution, the doctor agreed that any emotional feelings Ryan had expressed concerned fear for the consequences of his act. Everything he did after the killing was aimed at protecting himself.

Mr Rees asked the doctor: 'Being objective, you can no longer hold the opinion that on the balance of probability he was suffering from abnormality of the mind?'

Dr Nam replied: 'Not on the evidence in court.'

Mr Rees: 'All the evidence indicates not a man suffering from a reactive anxiety depression who snapped, but a man who committed a murder thinking about what he was doing at the time, doesn't it?'

The doctor replied simply: 'Yes.'

On Thursday, 2 May 1991, the jury at Cardiff Crown Court retired to consider their verdict, taking nearly three hours to return with a verdict of guilty of murder.

Jailing Ryan for life, Mr Justice Simon Browne told him: 'The jury have convicted you on the most compelling evidence of a dreadful murder. The murder of a wife, alas, is not nowadays wholly uncommon.

'But this case has about it the horrific dimension that before killing her you took her to an incinerator and after killing her placed her body in it. Heaven only knows what agonies she might have suffered while there.'

Defence counsel, Mr Gerard Elias, QC, told the judge: 'Ryan will have to live with what he has done and the consequences of it and the shame he feels.'

He said that Ryan's admissions to the police of how he had disposed of the body – without which they would have had no shred of evidence – must have been some indication of his feelings of guilt, shame and remorse. After all, Mr Elias said, Ryan had told the police: 'I am just sorry for what's happened.'

When the verdict was announced, a member of Mrs Ryan's family shouted from the public gallery: 'Thank God for that.'

Ryan had robbed them of a body to bury, but relatives

planned to have a memorial service for Linda Ryan in All Saints Church, Barry.

It was a strange case. In one way it was banal and commonplace: husbands kill their wives every week of the year. But what gave it a rare dimension was the method of disposing of the body. It was reminiscent of the Nazis and the Holocaust – not on the same scale, of course, but in the casual manner in which a killer could dispose of the body of his victim.

Remember when the nurse asked who the 'Linda' was whose name was tattooed on his arm? Ryan had replied: 'She's no one.' For that alone he deserves to rot in jail.

11
HUDDERSFIELD'S 'NO BODIES' MURDER CASE

For those students of murder who like to keep a check on the statistics, a recent Yorkshire trial made its small contribution to criminal history. Although eleventh in our series of missing bodies, it was only the sixth case in England this century in which the defendants were convicted of murder without the evidence of a body. In fact, the killer's guilt hung by a fingernail – literally.

Previous convitions were: the *Veronica* mutineers in 1903, a man called Davidson (who killed his baby son) in 1934, James Camb in 1948, the Hosein brothers in 1970, and Ian Simms in 1989.

This new case involved a clash of cultures, and was motivated by religious scruples. Sharifan Bibi was nineteen and her marriage to a man had been 'arranged' by her family. However, she flouted Muslim tradition by running away from her husband to live with her lover, Hashmat Ali, aged forty-six. She was a British-born Muslim girl, whose orthodox parents had emigrated to Huddersfield from rural Pakistan in 1968.

Huddersfield, lying at the heart of the Heavy Woollen District, has always been a wool textile town. Now the centre of the newly formed Metropolitan District of Kirklees, it boasts within its purlieus the reputed grave of Robin Hood, and in the early 1800s was the focal point of the Luddite Rebellion. It has a large Asian community, drawn to the town in the past by the promise of jobs in the mills – mills which have long since closed, victims of competition from cheap cloth from third-world countries.

Sharifan Bibi, despite her name, was 'Westernized'. Born in this country, she was, by any view, an Englishwoman. She was fashion-conscious and adored pop music. Bowing to the wishes of her father, she had been through an arranged marriage when she was sixteen, and again a couple of years later. But she was unhappy. She had grown up as a typical English girl, attending Moor End High School and then joining a youth training scheme where she was in contact with other teenagers. She believed in the customs of Britain; in particular, she wanted a relationship based on love.

She met and fell in love with Hashmat Ali, twenty-six years her senior, and moved in with him. By doing so she unwittingly signed her own death warrant. The couple shared a house in Elmwood Avenue, Huddersfield, and enjoyed a harmonious partnership. Hashmat Ali had children from a previous marriage, but they quickly took to the young Sharifan. It was her own family who were outraged by her behaviour, incensed to the point of murder . . .

In mid-December 1988 – just six weeks after they had begun living together – the couple vanished mysteriously from their home. Mr Ali's sons were concerned enough to call in the police, who broke into the house and found a puzzling scene. The lights were on. Fresh food was in the refrigerator, and all the family valuables were in the house. Even the couple's outdoor clothes were hanging neatly in the porch. And yet there was no sign of the occupants, and no neighbours had seen or heard anything unusual. Somehow the couple had been spirited away . . .

The sons suspected foul play from the start, based on the fact that their father had not collected his Christmas wages of £260, and Sharifan had failed to cash a social security cheque.

Based on the evidence before them, the police, too,

strongly suspected foul play and began a major investigation.

Detectives involved in the inquiry discovered that Mr Ali's red Peugeot had been found in London, in Heathrow Airport staff car park, on 26 February. Anxious to establish whether the couple had returned to Pakistan – which could not be ruled out – the police travelled to that country and questioned the families of both missing persons. Neither family had seen their kin, but one of them had something of interest to say. Two brothers of the missing woman had visited Pakistan after the couple had vanished, and one had told his relatives quite bluntly that 'we' had killed the couple and scattered their remains in ditches around Huddersfield. The reason given was the sister's behaviour, which had shamed the family. The witness was prepared to testify, and this was enough for the police.

The officer in charge of the inquiry, Detective Superintendent Tony Ridley, had already learned that Ali had received veiled threats from Sharifan's family to end the relationship, which outraged them. He had also discovered that Ali had probably met Sharifan through one of his two sons. For six years, until 1975, he had lived with an Englishwoman, and had two sons by her: Akhtar Preece and Mohammed Akram.

Sharifan's brothers, Mohammed Saleem, aged thirty-two, of Croydon, London, and twenty-six-year-old Abdul Haq, of Huddersfield, were the prime suspects in the case, and they were duly arrested and charged with the murders of the missing couple 'sometime between 18 December 1988 and 10 June 1990'. The charge was vague enough in its terms – an eighteen-month span for the murders – and, without any bodies, it seemed that a conviction was well-nigh impossible. However, the prosecution pressed on. The fifty-five-year-old father had also been arrested, but at the preliminary hearing the case against him was dismissed because of 'insufficient evidence'.

The police had been busy building up their case against the two brothers, using forensic archaeologists and other experts to bolster what little practical evidence they had. The case was always going to depend on circumstantial evidence, but as many a judge has reminded a jury, sometimes circumstantial evidence can be more compelling than direct evidence. It can form a chain of evidence which leads to only one logical conclusion.

The three-week trial of the brothers took place at Leeds Crown Court, commencing on Monday, 25 November 1991. For the prosecution, Mr Norman Jones, QC, began by telling the jury the background to the case. He suggested that the two brothers in the dock had killed the couple 'probably to protect the honour of the family, which, they felt, had been despoiled'. He said the family felt that their nineteen-year-old married sister, by living in adultery with a married man, offended them, in particular their religious father, who taught at a local mosque.

But Mr Jones admitted frankly: 'It is a very unusual case of murder for, whereas the Crown say these two people are dead, there are no bodies.'

He told of how, on 19 December 1988, Mrs Bibi and Mr Ali vanished from their Huddersfield home 'as though they had been spirited away from the Earth. The sons of Ali had found the couple missing, and the front door locked from the inside. A side door had been left open. They left behind a house with the lights on, there was fresh food in the fridge, and the phone off the hook.' Mr Jones said it was a very real mystery – adding: 'The couple abandoned everything they owned . . . The house was almost like the *Marie Celeste*, but instead of sailing it was standing still in Huddersfield. But like that ship, it was mute evidence of what had happened.'

Since everything the couple owned was still in the house, including their passports, with the lights on and the phone off the hook, the prosecution maintained that the couple had not left the house voluntarily, but had been 'abducted and killed'.

Mr Jones talked of the evidence which suggested murder. In November 1989 – a year after the alleged murders – workmen were called in to do some work in the cellar of a house belonging to Haq at 18 Crossland Road, Huddersfield. The police had not known of the existence of this house – Thornton Lodge – when they began their inquiry, and did not learn about it for several months, and then after a tip-off – but the workmen remembered clearly that the house had smelled of death. Mr Barry Riley, the builder, said that it 'stunk of dead animals'. He had been employed to concrete over the cellar floor. The prosecution claimed that the bodies had lain in a pit in the cellar for some time, weeks or months, prior to being moved.

When the police searched the house in Crossland Road, they discovered a freshly dug pit in the cellar. Dr John Hunter, a Bradford University archaeologist, had excavated the five-foot pit, sifting through the debris as it was removed. No bodies were unearthed. However, a human fingernail was found among the debris, and the police felt certain that the bodies had been in that pit at some stage.

Following the discovery of the car at Heathrow Airport, Detective Sergeant Peter Brook and Police Constable Rashid Awan were sent to Pakistan to make inquiries, and discovered that one of the brothers had told relatives in that country about killing their adulterous sister. They had even repeated their story to a grandfather. Mr Jones said that possibly Saleem had felt safe in talking about the murders to a member of his own family, thousands of miles from where the crime took place. But a cousin who had heard the confession would be among the prosecution witnesses.

With that, the Crown began calling its witnesses. Among the first was a younger brother of the two men in the dock. He said that ten months after his sister had vanished, Haq returned home one day with dirty shoes and clothing. The witness said he smelled 'like a dead cat' and began taking frequent baths. This, the prosecution claimed, indicated that he had been engaged in moving the bodies from the cellar.

The defendants' cousin, Mr Hussain, said that the defendants had stayed with him in Pakistan one night in early 1989, and Saleem told him he had killed the couple, disposing of their bodies in ditches. He agreed that when telling a policeman in Pakistan about the confession, he had not used the term 'we', but now remembered that Saleem had said 'we' killed them.

Mr Ullah, the grandfather, said that when told about the confession, he had questioned Saleem. The grandfather told the court: 'At first he kept quiet. Then he told me he had finished her.' Saleem had said the man living with his sister had been killed also.

Builder Mr Barry Riley told the court that when working in the cellar at Haq's house in November 1989, he and his men had had to take regular breaks for fresh air because of the foul and obnoxious smell inside. It was like nothing he had ever known before, and clung to his clothing and tools. Haq had explained the smell away by saying it was a broken drain. The prosecution claimed it was rotting flesh from the bodies in the pit.

A Home Office pathologist, Dr Siva, told the court of helping excavate the pit in the cellar and sifting through the debris. He had only found one human fingernail – and a glove which had a strong and offensive smell. He said: 'It reminded me of a body in a severe state of decomposition.' He said that during his twenty-five years' experience he had smelled that odour many times. It was an odour which could cling to materials for various lengths of time. It was the smell of death . . .

A pathologist called by the defence, Dr John Dossett, was asked by Mr Marron, defending Saleem, if two bodies – even if chopped up – could have fitted into that small pit found in the cellar. The pathologist said he doubted that the bodies would have fitted – 'It would have been a very tight squeeze' – and said in his opinion the smell in the cellar was not from decomposing flesh but from decaying vegetable matter. Had the chopped-up bodies been placed in plastic bags, he would have expected the bags to have burst because of the gases from the decomposing bodies, leaving traces of human material behind in the pit.

Towards the end of the trial, the defence called a witness who claimed to have seen the vanished couple six days after they were alleged to have been killed. He said he had been driving along and saw Mr Ali following him in his distinctive red car. 'I recognized him through my driving mirror.' The prosecution claimed the man was mistaken.

The defence began their case, with Mr Simon Hawkesworth, QC, defending Haq, telling the jury that there was no evidence to support the Crown case. There was not even evidence that the couple mentioned as victims were in fact dead. He went on to say that just because Haq was a Muslim did not mean he would kill his sister for her adultery. Haq had made it clear to the police that his religion included the concept of forgiveness.

'We say there is no evidence to support the suggestion that anyone in that household, let alone Abdul Haq, was so under the influence of his father that he would go out to commit murder to uphold the family name.'

Mr Marron, for Saleem, told the jury in his closing speech that far from being a strict Muslim, Saleem was himself a womanizer. 'He wouldn't kill for adultery because he has engaged in it so often himself.'

In his closing speech for the prosecution, Mr Jones reminded the jury that it was almost the third anniversary of the couple's disappearance. 'The Crown say from that day to this, there has been no credible sighting of either of them.'

The jury deliberated for a long time over this case,

taking five hours, including an overnight stay in a hotel, before returning on Tuesday, 17 December 1991, with unanimous verdicts of guilty of murder against both brothers. In mitigation, counsel for Saleem said it had been a family matter, and there was no suggestion that there was any risk from Saleem in the future.

The trial judge, Mr Justice Ian Kennedy, was unmoved by this. Sentencing both men to life imprisonment, he reminded them firmly: 'You are members of a wider family, the family of the human race. That is a point that must be remembered. The sentence upon you each is life imprisonment.'

As he was led away Haq shouted: 'There is no justice. It's a kangaroo court.'

But justice it was, even without the bodies. While an acquittal would not have surprised anyone listening to the case, the jury heard all the evidence and searched their consciences, applying common sense to the facts in the case.

Muslims in Britain have been divided by this case. A community-relations worker in Huddersfield, where the 123,000 population includes 13,000 Muslims of Pakistani origin commented: 'Most first-generation Muslim men in West Yorkshire will back the brothers. They may not approve of the killings, but they will be understanding.'

But a local religious leader, Mr Shafi Chopdfat, stated: 'Do not use this case to attack the whole Muslim community. Islam preaches non-violence. Killing a person has nothing to do with religion.'

This case, adding as it does to the file on murder convictions without a body, is indeed a triumph for justice. In Britain even the 'vanished' have the right to that.

12
VARIOUS ATTEMPTS TO DESTROY THE BODY . . .

Ever since man began killing, he began trying to hide the evidence of his deed: the body itself. Every conceivable method has been tried over the ages: burning, dismemberment, secret burial on land or at sea, dissolving in acid, hiding in attics, and so on.

In 1725 Catherine Hayes had her husband dismembered, his head being thrown into the Thames. However, it was washed ashore and her crime quickly discovered. She was burned alive at the stake for *petty treason:* husband murder. In 1849 Professor John White Webster killed fellow-academic Dr George Parkman following a row over money. He cut him up in his laboratory at Massachusetts Medical College and burned the body in an assay oven. But an inquisitive janitor found the remains of the body burning in the oven – the teeth were still intact. Webster was hanged on 30 August 1850. John George Haigh tried acid; his victim's gallstones and acrylic dentures betrayed him. Brian Donald Hume tried dropping the pieces from an aircraft, following dismemberment. James Camb used a ship's porthole, as we have seen. Dennis Nilsen flushed the pieces of his victims down the toilet.

In all such cases what brings the guilt home to the murderer is the *identification* of the victim. In a recent Welsh case, a man named Perry attempted to cook away the evidence of his crime. John Perry, aged fifty-two, from Clwyd, had married a young and pretty Filipino girl, Arminda, and brought her back to this country. But she began an affair with a neighbour and demanded a divorce, which would have ruined Perry financially. In February 1991 he killed her. The police arrested Perry at his home on 28 February, and when they asked where his wife was, Perry pointed to two plastic carrier bags. Inside the bags were the cooked remains of his wife. Perry told officers: 'I fed some of her to the cat.'

Perry admitted spending twelve hours cutting his wife up in the bath – 'dicing her up', as he put it – and he took another three days to cook his wife's body, removing the eyes and brain from her baked skull to scatter over nearby fields. At his trial at Mold Crown Court, beginning on 19 November 1991, the prosecution said that the process of dismemberment and cooking was to conceal the evidence of the crime by destroying the identity of the victim. Perry claimed he had killed his twenty-seven-year-old wife accidently, following a struggle after a row, but the trial judge asked him: 'Mr Perry, why did you put your wife's head in the oven?' It must be a classic judicial ironic remark. The head had been cooked at the highest setting for eight hours.

Perry said he had made his choice on strictly scientific criteria. After all, the human body consists mainly of water, and cooking would evaporate that water and leave only a fraction of the body to be disposed of – or so he had thought.

The prosecutor told of how detectives who called at Perry's bungalow were struck by the smell of roasting meat, which permeated the house, and by the fact that every surface was covered with a film of grease. Open on a coffee-table was a medical encyclopaedia showing diagrams of the human body. The police also found a note in Perry's handwriting which detailed how much he would save by murdering his wife. It read: '*Save £3,799 without divorce and re-mortgage, £72.67 per week, or £315 per month*.' It had not been a crime of passion, as Perry claimed; the motive had been sordid greed.

Mr Carlile, prosecuting, told the jury that although Perry had disposed of much of his wife's remains, the police visit had caught him with enough remains still in his possession to convict him. He added that the disposal process had been so meticulous that a Home Office pathologist had been unable to determine the cause or exact date of the wife's death. The implication was that given another week or so, Perry might have got clean away with it.

A workmate had advised Perry that 'it didn't take long to butcher a carcass with good knives if you followed the seams of the joints, Mr Carlile said, and although Perry admitted strangling his wife, the prosecution did not accept that as being true. 'One of the reasons for cutting her up was to conceal how violently she had died.'

Perry would claim it had been an impulsive act, a crime of passion provoked by jealousy, but the evidence showed a keen and cold intelligence at work. Mr Carlile said: 'When the police arrived at Perry's house, a lot of cleaning and washing up was being done.' But Perry had failed to destroy the forensic evidence.

Mr Carlile said that a forensic scientist, Mrs Sarah Brownhill, had 'found evidence to indicate that an attack took place in the living room while the person being attacked was actually lying on the carpet'. She had examined tools, including an electric drill, hammer, chisels, a saw and junior hacksaw, and found that some had traces of blood, hair and muscle tissue, and there were fragments of ground bone in the jaws of the drill chuck.

On the second day of the trial Home Office pathologist Dr Donald Wayte told of how, when he arrived at the Perrys' home, he had been confronted with the smell of 'a Sunday roast – as if someone had cooked a beef'. He was shown carrier bags and plastic bins, dispersed around the bungalow, which contained varying amounts of diced, sawn or drilled human flesh, bones and tissue, the majority of which had been roasted in a double oven.

Dr Wayte later achieved a partial reconstruction of the skeleton, but said that the arrangement of the body parts in the bungalow had been 'extremely orderly . . . One would say that whoever had done it was almost obsessional, a very tidy person keeping everything together. There was no mess or anything. It had been carefully done. The cooked flesh had been cut into regular blocks. It was so uniform it was as if someone was preparing a stew.'

Of the skull found in a carrier bag, Dr Wayte said that it had been cut into four pieces with a drill. There were about forty holes. All the bones and flesh had been cooked at about 450° F – the highest setting on Perry's oven.

Mr Dombrowski, a former workmate of Perry's, went into the witness box to tell of how, only five weeks prior to the murder, he had given Perry details of how to butcher and bone a carcass. He said he had been bragging when he claimed he could complete work on a carcass in twenty minutes, but he went on: 'I told him how to do a carcass: boning out and scraping. I just said you go down the seams . . . get sharp knives.' Mr Dombrowski revealed that he had also told Perry about the similarity between cooked pork and human flesh. During an earlier conversation, Perry had suggested that someone 'could easily get away with a body' by using the vat of acid in a neighbouring factory.

Inspector Ross Duffield said that together with Sergeant Derek Frost, he had visited Perry's home in February because of concern about his missing wife. He told the court: 'The first thing I was struck by was a pungent smell somewhere near the smell of cooked meat. It was so pungent I felt I could taste it.' He said that at first 'Mr Perry was calm and lucid in conversation and seemed unconcerned about his wife's disappearance, but when told we would have to search the house, I noticed a change. He became uneasy and shuffled in his seat.' After a few more questions he had begun showing the officers his wife's remains in various bags. In the garage he had pointed to one bag and commented: 'I've fed some of her to the cat.'

The garage, Inspector Duffield said, had had a bad smell. 'There was an awful smell – perhaps even worse, there was the smell of putrid flesh as well as burnt flesh.'

Perry had been arrested and taken to Mold police station in handcuffs. At the police station he had told Sergeant Andrew Hunter, who booked him in: 'I've done a good turn. I fed her to the animals.'

Perry went into the witness box to tell his own story, claiming he had strangled his wife following a row. He removed the clothing from the body, then took it into the bathroom, where he began dismembering it. He said he severed his wife's head and shaved her hair off, then cooked it in the oven, hoping it would make it easier to get the skull open. After cooking it, he drilled and sawed it open. Inside was a 'grey slurry' which he poured into a bucket. He said he dissolved much of the brain, which he described as 'like grease and fat', in Ariel liquid. He said he also put the eyes in the bucket, which he then buried in the countryside.

Then had come his frequent trips, back and forth, disposing of the blood by the bucketful in woods nearby his home. But even now he claimed: 'I didn't know what I was doing. I wasn't in control of my faculties.'

In cross-examination, Mr Carlile asked Parry if he agreed that his conduct was 'completely and inexcusably unreasonable'.

Perry replied: 'Not for killing her. Afterwards I didn't know what I was doing.'

Mr Carlile pressed: 'Why did you cook her?'

Perry replied: 'I knew from when I was a schoolboy that the body comprises approximately seven-tenths water, and that if I removed the water I could disperse the body in shallow graves around the countryside and it would never be found.' It was like a bright, earnest schoolboy explaining a basic scientific principle. To him, it seemed perfectly logical. If ever there was proof of disassociation, this was it. Even in the witness box, Perry didn't realize how ghoulish he sounded.

He went on: 'I had actually severed the head. As it was, it was heated in the oven.'

This was too much for the judge, who wanted to know how Perry could claim 'it was all rather a blank' and yet could remember precise details. Mr Justice Scott-Baker asked: 'Mr Perry, why did you put your wife's head in the oven?'

Perry replied: 'I didn't know about the temperatures at which bones cooked. I soon discovered it wouldn't reduce the bones . . . The reason for putting the other things there was to get rid of the water.' He said he had gone backward and forward, taking something like twenty gallons of diluted blood to sprinkle over nearby forestry land and adjacent fields and ditches.

He agreed with the prosecutor that he had 'swilled her out all over the countryside'. He also said that the entire process of dismemberment had taken twelve hours.

On 26 November Perry was convicted and sentenced to life imprisonment, after the jury had deliberated for five hours and fifteen minutes, returning with a ten to two majority verdict.

Sentencing him to life behind bars, the judge told Perry: 'You initially tried to have your wife thrown out of Britain by telling the immigration officials a pack of lies. When that failed, your mind turned to the possibility that one day you might kill her.

'Last February, in the small hours of the morning, you lost your temper and did just that. You then set about dismembering her mortal remains with a chilling and ruthless efficiency, which included cooking most of the pieces. There is evidence that had you not been arrested, those pieces would have disappeared for ever in the acid tanks at your place of work. You have not shown one scrap of remorse . . .'

After the case, detectives involved in the inquiry called the murder 'the most gruesome and inhuman in British criminal history'. Detective Superintendent Cooke said: 'The smell in the bungalow is one thing that will stay with me for ever. My colleagues and I have attended many murders, and we recognized the smell of death. But this was the most gruesome thing any of us had ever come across: someone actually roasting a body as they would a Sunday joint . . . It was almost unbelievable. Even the pathologist, on being given a verbal account, doubted that we had human remains.

'As the detective in charge of the investigation, I remain intrigued as to why he went to such lengths to desecrate this body. Even the serial killers in America haven't gone to these lengths . . .

'I suspect that this case is almost unique in this country – and not a matter we would look forward to dealing with again . . . It's difficult to imagine the mind that could do this to another human being. Had the officers not called, it is doubtful that we would have recovered any of the remains.' He added: 'I believe this may well have been an attempt to commit the perfect murder.'

While not decrying any of the excellent work done by the police in this case, much of what the officer in charge said is well over the top and displays a surprising naivety. There have been far worse murders – one only has to think of Dennis Nilsen butchering his fifteen victims. And it isn't the first time a body has been roasted. A graduate disposed of his wife in London in that same manner a few years ago, scattering her remains in plastic bags all over the city. And as for American serial killers, there is *nothing* they haven't done . . .

Twenty-five-year-old John David was convicted in December 1988 of the murder of his girlfriend Miriam Jones, having disposed of her body at an isolated pig farm near Maidenhead. He had set the body on fire with petrol, then left it for the pigs to devour – an echo of the McKay case. The prosecution revealed that 'partly gnawed human bones and a few scraps of the dead woman's clothing were recovered from deep in the mud, and from the pigs themselves'. David was duly sentenced to life imprisonment.

Perhaps the days of the missing *corpus delecti* are over. Forensic science has advanced to the point where it may prove impossible ever to fully destroy the body of the victim – as the following case of the 'skinned torso' demonstrates. The evidence uncovered by a patient pathologist and determined detectives was as 'cogent and compelling' as any identity card.

It was always going to be a headache for the police and forensic experts. A headless torso, which had been expertly skinned, found in a forest grave, the only clues being the curtains in which the limbless body was wrapped, and two nightdresses used to carry the other parts.

The woman's body was found by a motorist at a lay-by on the busy A22 in the Ashdown Forest, between Nutley and Wych Cross, on Sunday, 31 August 1986. The pieces were in two shallow graves about five feet apart and covered with a layer of earth and bracken. It was the revolting smell which had aroused the motorist's attention. One grave contained the torso, minus the arms and head. The legs had been severed at the knees. The other grave contained further remains and a nightdress. The head and hands were missing, but most horribly, the body had been expertly skinned like a rabbit to remove identifying marks such as scars or tattoos.

Dr Michael Heath, a forensic pathologist at the London Hospital, spent some days examining the remains and was able to report that the victim was a woman aged about thirty, who had probably been butchered about eleven days before she was found, which meant she would have been murdered over the August Bank Holiday weekend.

The medical evidence suggested that the woman had given birth at least once, and she had a prominent rib and a vaginal scar, but there was no evidence of sexual assault. The killer had removed all the internal organs, apart from the heart and lungs, from the torso. The dissection had been carried out with some surgical skill.

On 17 September the police had put two dummies on display, one wearing a pink negligée, the other a pale lemon nightdress, with the blue floral curtains as a backcloth. They were shown on the BBC TV programme *Crimewatch UK*, in the hope that a viewer might recognize the items of clothing. A woman viewer contacted the police as a result. She was certain she had sold the curtains at a car-boot sale in Crawley in October 1985. She was able to describe the woman purchaser.

Detective Superintendent Bryan Grove was the officer in charge of the case. Never before in his thirty years in the force had he come across a body with no fingerprints, a skull, or even skin. But when asked at a press conference if this could be the 'perfect murder', he replied gruffly: 'There is no such thing. We know that she is nearer thirty than twenty years old. She was white with a slight tan and of medium build, about five feet three inches tall. She has had a baby, but we are not sure when. We know her blood group.'

Dr Michael Heath added: 'The killer has not done that good a job in terms of destroying identity. We know quite a lot already, and we are getting closer to age with tests on the bones. I have established a form of death, but the police do not wish to disclose this information yet. I would say whoever did this murder had quite a considerable understanding of how a body fitted together. It is a hard job to take a body apart. It would have taken at least half a day. This is quite a challenge

– it always is with dismembered bodies – but eventually the process is very revealing.'

The revelations were initiated by the killer himself, panicked by the press reports of police progress in the case. On 28 October a Moroccan named Kassem Lachaal went to his solicitor in Crawley asking him to contact the police to tell them that his younger wife, twenty-five-year-old Latifa Lazaar, was missing. (Under Muslim law he could have two wives.) He said he feared she was the victim found in Ashdown Forest and that blame might be put on him.

This was the break the police had been waiting for. They moved into the closely-knit Moroccan community in Crawley, asking questions. They discovered that Kassem Lachaal had an unsavory reputation as a womanizer, having had at least a dozen affairs with other men's wives. More significantly, he was already on police files. He had been released from prison in 1986, after serving a sentence for drug-smuggling, and his date of release was just days prior to the murder.

Lachaal lived with his number one wife, Fatima, at one house, while his second wife, Latifa, lived with their son at another house. Lachaal divided his life between the two women. The police now searched the house in which Latifa had lived, finding forensic traces indicating that someone had been cut up in the bath. Officers flew to Morocco to take blood samples from the missing woman's relatives, and were able to establish from the DNA fingerprint test that the skinned torso was indeed that of Latifa Lazaar. There was a clear relationship between the blood from the torso and that of the relatives.

Both Lachaal and his first wife were tried for murder at Lewes Crown Court on 29 February 1988, both the accused pleading not guilty. Just prior to the trial the missing skull of the victim was found in undergrowth near the school where she had worked. Dr Heath was able to link this to the torso.

The prosecution told the jury that the dead woman had last been seen alive with Lachaal the day before she was murdered. Forensic evidence indicated that Latifa had been butchered in her own home. The prosecutor stated: 'In the course of time she was cut up and butchered.' Forensic scientist David Northcott testified that he had found a total of 140 bloodstains in the bathroom of the murder house.

'The bloodstains and their distribution was consistent with violence having taken place in that bathroom,' he said. 'Someone was injured in that room and was losing blood, and that had been spread around by violent acts.'

It truly was a case where the evidence was written in blood. The blood, the scientist said, was of Latifa's blood group. 'None of the stains could have come from either of the two accused.'

Neighbours testified to having seen the two accused loading bulky plastic plastic bin-liners into their car around the time of the murder.

On the sixth day of the trial relatives from Morocco told of having received letters from Latifa which had evidently been forged. One said that she was leaving her husband to marry '*a good-looking Pakistani. I know what I am doing. Don't worry about me. I am happy now.*'

A social worker said the first wife had broken down one day and told her: 'I wish we hadn't done it.' The social worker said she had felt 'too stunned' to go on with the conversation.

In his closing speech the prosecutor said that jealousy and tensions had built up with two women sharing the same husband. He said that Latifa was killed because 'the cauldron was bubbling and something was ready to boil over'.

On Thursday, 24 March 1988 the jury retired, taking almost seven hours to find Kassem Lachaal guilty of murdering his wife. It was a ten to two majority verdict.

The jury convicted Fatima of helping conceal the crime, but acquitted her of murder. Kassem was jailed for life, the wife to eighteen months' imprisonment.

The couple were removed from the dock, marking the end of an eighteen-day trial during which the jury had listened to details of the most grisly murder in the recent history of Sussex. But it was a murder solved by science. The killer had been cunning, skinning the victim and removing those parts which could identify her: the hands and head. But he could not fool the scientists. Forensic science is the tool which will see the end of attempts to hide the body. It just can't be done . . .

However, there is a footnote to all this. Readers may wonder if it is possible to completely dispose of a human body, especially in the middle of a crowded city. A recent case may help decide the issue.

On 12 June 1992, a man was jailed for life at the Old Bailey for the murders of two young women whose bodies were never found. Thomas King, aged forty-three, dismembered the bodies of Barbara Hunt, who was twenty-seven, and Joanne Rankin, who was twenty-three, in the bath at his shared flat. David Waters, prosecuting, told the Recorder of London, Judge Lawrence Verney, that King stated he had left the pieces – which have never been recovered – in rubbish bins on the south London estate where he lived.

The police spent twenty-two days searching rubbish tips as a result of King's confession, but no trace of the bodies was ever found – although both women had indeed mysteriously vanished.

King, a former chef and butcher, of Glasbury Estate, Stockwell, who trained as a chef at Harrods in the 1960s, confessed his crimes to the police after being arrested while attempting to kill another woman, Margaret Horner.

King told the police that he had no remorse for attacking Miss Horner, saying: 'My one regret was she never died. I felt afterwards I did a bad job and I intended to go out and do a good job.'

King pleaded guilty to murdering Miss Hunt between 7 September and 16 October 1991, and Miss Rankin between 18 September and 16 October, and to wounding Nicola Corner with intent, both on or about 16 October 1991. He had been high on a cocktail of drugs on both occasions.

Mr Waters described how, at midnight on 15 October 1991, Miss Horner reached the door of her home in Brixton, south London, when she felt a hand on her shoulder and a knife at her throat. A man's voice growled: 'Don't scream or I'll kill you.' She was then attacked with the knife before Miss Corner, who lived at the same address, went to her aid and was herself attacked.

Mr Waters said that if Miss Corner had given evidence, she would have described how King 'just stared at us. He was manic-looking.' King then ran off, but was arrested nearby, covered in blood and still carrying his knife. He admitted the attacks and told the police that he had sharpened his knife to a razor-edge 'to kill somebody' and, showing it to the police, he said: 'It's lovely, isn't it?' He also told them: 'I wanted to be looked after by the State.'

Mr Waters went on: 'He said he tried to kill the woman so he would go to prison for a long time where he could be looked after by the State.'

Once in custody, King admitted both murders, telling the police that Miss Hunt had sought refuge at his flat on the night of 8 September 1991. She was drunk, following a row with her boyfriend, and King had offered her a bed for the night. 'He cut her throat while she slept on a mattress in his living room,' Mr Waters said. 'It took him two and a half days to dismember the body.' He had left the corpse under a pile of dirty washing in the bath, but kept the taps running to hide any smell.

Mr Waters told the court that two other men had used the same bathroom, unaware of the body in the bath. King told the police that he had killed the woman whose body he cut up in his bath because 'I was washing up in the kitchen when I had this feeling her life was a mess and she sold herself for a can of drink. She had a bad name round the estate. I brought some peace to her . . . '

King had met Miss Rankin at Brixton tube station and taken her to his flat, where he killed her in the early hours of 20 September 1991, cutting her throat on the same mattress with the same five-inch-bladed knife. This time he took only three hours to dismember the body. He used his butcher's skills to cut the body into tiny pieces, which he stuffed into bin bags and threw down a communal waste-disposal shaft.

King told detectives: 'The bodies were not much of a problem to me. They just seemed like another carcass.' He also revealed that he had stolen seventy pence from one of his victims, which he used to buy a tin of cat food. 'I remember thinking it was a cheap price for a life,' he said.

Describing his feelings prior to his murders, King told detectives: 'I would say I was in a normal frame of mind. I go out at night when the streets are quiet and peaceful. That night, one minute I was there in the kitchen, the next I was there, all of a sudden like.'

Sentencing King to concurrent life sentences for the murders and attempted murder, and five years for the wounding, the judge said: 'It is apparent that a Mental Health Act disposal would not be appropriate.'

Such a case is truly chilling.

The question I am most often asked during interviews is: 'Why are you so fascinated with murder?' My reply is always the same: that the best way to take the pulse of any society is to study the nature of its crimes at any particular point in time. And on that basis, ours is a very sick society indeed . . .

We are breeding creatures like King – savage reptiles who only come out at night – faster than we can lock them away. But the really disturbing feature about this case is that but for King's confession, the fate of those two young women would never have been known. It is indeed possible to completely dispose of a human body – even in the middle of a capital city.

BIBLIOGRAPHY

Bishop, Jim. *The Murder Trial of Judge Peel.* Trident Press, New York. (1963)

Boucher, Anthony. *The Quality of Murder*. Dutton, New York. (1962)

Casswell, J. D. *A Lance for Liberty*. Harrap. (1961)

Cooper, William. *Shall We Ever Know?* Hutchinson. (1971)

Deale, Kenneth. *Memorable Irish Trials*. Constable. (1960)

Deeley, Peter, & Walker, Christopher. *Murder In The Fourth Estate*. Gollancz. (1971)

Duncan, Ronald. *Facets of Crime*. Bossiney Books, Cornwall. (1975)

Franklin, Charles. *The Woman in The Case*. Robert Hale. (1967)

Furneaux, Rupert. *Famous Criminal Cases 2*. Allan Wingate. (1955)

Godwin, John. *Killers Unknown*. Herbert Jenkins. (1960)

Humphreys, Sir Travers. *A Book of Trials*. Heinemann. (1953)

Jones, Frank. *Murderous Women*. Headline. (1990)

Kelly, Vince. *The Shark Arm Case*. Angus & Robertson. Sydney. (1963)

Laurence, J. *Extraordinary Crimes*. Sampson Low Marston. (1931)

Lucas, Norman. *The Murder of Muriel McKay*. Arthur Barker (1971)

Symons, Julian. *Beyond a Reasonable Doubt*. Cressett Press. (1960)

Thomas, David. *Seek Out the Guilty*. John Long. (1960)

Wagner, Diane. *Corpus Delecti*. St Martin's Press, New York. (1986)

Whitelaw, David. *Corpus Delecti*. Geoffrey Bles. (1936) *Notable British Trials*. William Hodge. (eighty-three titles)

INDEX